# THE BOX OF THE COVENANT

## Unbelievable Journey of a Young Maid in Pursuit of her Education Dreams

GEMMA

authorHOUSE®

*AuthorHouse™ UK*
*1663 Liberty Drive*
*Bloomington, IN 47403  USA*
*www.authorhouse.co.uk*
*Phone: 0800.197.4150*

*Published by AuthorHouse   08/02/2018*

*ISBN: 978-1-5462-8695-0 (sc)*
*ISBN: 978-1-5462-8694-3 (e)*

# DEDICATION

To all faithful maids and house girls in the world, continue to be faithful and work hard. For those who have dreams, keep on dreaming and focus to make sure your dream becomes reality. Do not lose focus, though you might encounter things that will make you feel you are nothing. For those who believe you don't have dreams, I say you actually do. Don't live like someone whose life has no meaning. You are very special and significant in this life. You are carrying God's purpose. So take yourself serious, knowing that we are all equal and that a person's life worth is not measured by the abundance of his or her material possessions.

Serve with loyalty and respect your employers even though sometimes they might mistreat you. Never do anything bad to them or their children, and God, who is the giver of life, will reward you. For Bible readers, always remember Romans 12:19, which reads, "Do not take revenge, my dear friends, but leave room for God's wrath, for it is written: 'It is mine to avenge; I will repay,' says the Lord."

To employers and anyone who is in charge of people, treat people as you wish to be treated. Treat people with the same love and respect you wish to receive from them. Never take advantage of anybody; you don't know why that person is working for you, and you don't know who that person will be in the future. For bosses who mistreat maids and house girls, please do not continue to mistreat them, as they are weak and voiceless. Instead, empower them so that they will be able to help themselves and help others, I believe that is how human beings are meant to treat each other. My husband once said, "When you are strong, it's for the weak, and when you are rich, it's for the poor."

To the refuges in the world, who are running from various disasters, keep on running, believing tomorrow will not be the same. If at some point in your life you had a dream to be somebody, keep on dreaming. Never let your dream fade away as a result of any situation or circumstance. Keep on! Keep on moving. The future is bright; the future is great. Make sure that, one day, your dream becomes reality. I am saying this because once I was on the run, and though my circumstances may have been different, the goal might be the same.

To students of all levels, never give up on your studies. You can do and achieve anything if you believe, determined and discipline yourself. Just commit yourself, focus, and work hard. Then you will see the fruits of your commitment to your studies. As the old adage says, "Where there is a will, there is a way." If I did it, you can do it.

To marginalised people, especially young girls and women, fight for freedom and access to opportunities. When the opportunities come, do your best to maximise them. Don't listen to the discouraging voices that say you can't do it or that you will never make it in life. Never despair, have faith, and hold on even when things seem hopeless. One day, things will turn in your favour.

To my children, I have written this book to remind you of the divine power of God, who revealed himself to Moses as I am who I am. He has been with me throughout my life; I have never seen Him failing me. Please seek Him day and night. Then your life will be prosperous wherever you go.

# FOREWORD

The world is full of new possibilities if we push our limitations out of the way. This book is not just another life story; rather, it's a book in which the writer has put down life lessons that will not only inspire someone but also give readers tools that can be useful in various life endeavours. The writer has narrated her life experiences to give hope and new light, not only to those who go through difficult circumstances but also to those with dreams and aspirations to pursue greatness.

Through *The Box of the Covenant*, the writer has unfolded yet another truth—that, through diligence and determination, anyone can achieve the unthinkable and do the impossible. I can easily conclude that *impossible* is just a word, which you can change if you work hard to delete the first two letters. The readers of the bestselling book in the world can recall this line: "Nothing is impossible to the one who believes."

-Her Great Supporter

# ACKNOWLEDGEMENTS

First and foremost, I would like to acknowledge God, who is the source of my life and strength. Thank you for your divine love and grace upon my life. Without your sacrificial love, I would not be alive today to write this book. Thank you for being so merciful even in my weaknesses.

To my husband, thank you so much for your support and encouragement and for pushing me so hard to write this book. Thank you for always reminding me about God's purpose in my life. Your support, love, and contribution are highly appreciated. You have taught and inspired me so much with your faith, integrity, and love for God. Continue to love and seek Him every day.

To my lovely two girls, thank you so much for allowing me to write this book. Thank you for bearing with me during all this time when I was so busy writing. You have been such wonderful and amazing girls. It's my prayer that God will always protect and guide you.

To my faithful and loving UK mum, thank you for encouraging me to write this book. Thank you for always reminding me how important this book is to people. You have touched my heart so much with your love and kindness. Often when we met, you showed me information on self-publishing; you have influenced me to write this book. Thank you.

To the late professor and his wife, this book is the product of your love and sacrifice. You gave me opportunity and trusted me beyond doubt. Your inspirational guidance and support has left a lasting memory in my life. Your legacy will last for generations.

To the Family that changed my life, you have been a part of my life. Through your children, the door was opened. I am truly grateful for your contribution and the role you have played in the transformation of my life. Thank you for allowing God to use you and your family to fulfil what He wanted in my life.

# CHAPTER 1

## LET NO ONE DECIDE HOW YOUR LIFE SHOULD BE AND END

I was born in Magwa, a small village in the Singida region of Tanzania, to a family of nine children. I am the seventh child. We were among the poor people in that village, living only on what we could get. My mother separated from my father when I was five years old. Thanks to God, my sisters, brothers, and I were raised by my grandmother for the first few years of my life. During my early childhood, our grandmother was strong and hard-working, and she could take good care of us.

However, when my grandmother became too old to take care of us, my siblings and I had to be with our mother. We lived in poverty and hardship. When I turned seven, the age for starting primary school in Tanzania, my mother refused to register me for school. She believed that it was a waste of time, since I would be married in the near future, and my bride price would contribute to the upkeep of the family.

Seeing my peers go to school while I was left at home was the most difficult and painful moment I experienced during that time. My friends did not understand why I was not going to school, so they tried to convince me to go with them. I told them I didn't want to go because I didn't like school, but that was a lie. Deep inside, I really wanted to attend school, but I was ashamed to tell them the truth—that my mum didn't want me to go to school.

In our culture, men, especially the old ones, made fun of young girls by calling them *mke wangu,* meaning "my wife". When I was seven years of age, I did not like anybody to call me wife. But it was not easy to avoid or go against, because society accepted it, and it seemed to be a way of life. Because I was not going to school, I faced even more of this mockery every single day. It affected me so much emotionally. It was annoying to be told that I was not supposed to attend school because I would soon get married.

One day two friends convinced me to go to school with them. They told me they were having fun at school. So without thinking twice, we arranged for them to pass by my house early next morning, so we could go to school together. The night after my friends and I made our plans, I asked my mother, "Mama, what will you do if one day I decide to go to school?"

"If you want to know what I will do to you, just try me," she replied.

I wanted to know what would happen after I left for school the next morning. But I did not care much about what she would do to me. I had already made up my mind and was looking forward to having fun with my friends at school.

The next day, which was Monday, I woke up early, while everybody else was still sleeping. I went out to wait for my friends. It did not take long before they came. On the way, I asked them if the teachers would allow me to get in the school, since I was not wearing a uniform. One of my friends replied, "Do not worry. Of course they will allow you."

A few minutes after we arrived at school, I heard the bell ringing and saw students from different classes running toward an open space. "Gemma, let's go," my friend told me. So I followed them. I did not know where we were going, but we were heading to that same open space where the other students were going.

When we got there, many students were already in lines according to their classes. "Get behind me," my friend told me. So I stood behind her, and we made a line. A few minutes later, men and women holding sticks came towards us. I bombarded her with questions about why the adults had sticks. "Stop asking questions. Be quiet. The teachers are coming now," she finally told me.

I was very scared. As the teachers approached, I noticed everybody was quiet, and I became even more scared.

About eight teachers came forward, but only one spoke. "If you know you are not in uniform, please come forward and tell us why you are not in uniform."

Her eyes were on me. I was the only one there without a uniform. My heart started to beat so fast, and my hands were sweating. I guessed that by "uniform" the teacher meant clothes and not everything we had on, or all of us would have been in trouble. Everybody had different shoes and different kinds of socks. Some did not even have shoes; at least I was wearing big sleepers.

The other students were looking at me and whispering, "Nenda mbele, nenda mbele!" ("Go forward, go forward!") Only my two friends were silent.

"Nenda mbele," one of the students said. "*Mwalimu*

*akikufuata fimbo zitaongezeka!*" ("If a teacher comes to you, the number of floggings will increase.")

I had to decide quickly. If I stepped forward without a uniform, I would be flogged; but if the teacher came to me, then I would be flogged even more. Therefore, I jumped to the front.

"Why are you not wearing a uniform?" the teacher asked.

"*Kwasababu ni siku ya kwanza kuja shule*" ("Because it is my first day at school"), I replied.

The teacher asked, "Where have you been all this time? It has been weeks since school started."

I did not have an answer, so I just kept quiet.

"Go back, and make sure you get registered and get a uniform."

I went back to my position in the line.

Then, after a few announcements, we went to class.

A few minutes later, the first teacher came in. He taught mathematics and was amazed at how I could understand things so quickly. He asked us to come to the front of the class to do some questions on the board. He told students who did not get the question right, "You have been here for weeks now, and you don't understand anything. Gemma just came today, and she can do better than you." He wasn't happy with their performance, but for me, I was very excited. I enjoyed everything we were doing, since it was my first time in a classroom.

After an hour, the first teacher left, and a second one came to teach us for the next hour. When the second bell rang, the teacher said, "*Nendeni mapumziko*" ("Go for the break"). Immediately, all the students left the classroom and went to play. Some ate their snacks before playing. I enjoyed every minute I spent with my fellow students because everybody was so friendly. Most of the students from my class wanted to play with me. Word had spread that I was intelligent, so they thought I would be good at playing as well, and they wanted me to play on their teams.

After the break, we went back to the classroom, and the third teacher came in. Before she started teaching, she asked the class, "Who is Gemma?"

Everybody went quiet, including me. I was so scared and wondered, *What have I done wrong?*

"I asked, who is Gemma in this classroom?" she repeated.

I raised my hand and said, "Here I am, Teacher."

"Ooh! So it's you! I heard you just came today, and you can do better than anyone else in this class. Where have you been all this time when other students were attending school?"

I was not able to give her an answer. I knew if I told the truth, I would have caused problems between my mother and the school. I did not want that to happen because I knew my mother very well, and she would make my life more miserable at home. So I just kept quiet, and the teacher told me to sit down.

She taught us for about an hour. Then the bell rang for the third time, and the students started singing, *"Kwaheri mwalimu tutaonana tena kesho"* ("Goodbye, teacher, we will see you again tomorrow").

After the song ended, the teacher left the class. My friends came to my desk and told me it was time to go home. Suddenly, I started sweating, and my heartbeat increased. I knew, when I get home, I would be punished for not obeying my mother. On the way, my friends kept asking me if I had fun and if I had changed my mind about attending school. *"Nitajua nikifika nyumbani"* ("I will know if I want to join or not when I get home"), I replied. Joining or not

5

joining the school would be determined by my mother's reaction when I get home.

When I reached home, I found my mother in the sitting room with her two friends. They were drinking traditional alcohol. I greeted them. Her friends responded, but my mother did not. Instead, she gave me a certain look, which I knew meant I was in trouble. "Where are you coming from?" my mom asked.

"From school," I replied.

She kept quiet.

A few minutes later, the friends left, and my mother escorted them out. When she came back, she was holding two sticks. She was extremely agitated, and she punished me severely.

After that day, I never tried again to go to school. Watching my friends and age-mates going to school while I was staying at home taking care of my brother and sister was sure difficult and painful, though. After that day, I stayed home, waiting for my mother to decide my fate. The only thing I was waiting for was for a man who was interested in me to appear and marry me, although I did not know when a person cruel enough to want to marry a little girl like me would show up. To my surprise, it did not take long time before that person appeared.

One day I was coming from the river where I'd fetched water. It was about 3 p.m. when I got home. Outside our house, I saw two cows and three men, who I greeted before I went into the house. Inside, I found an old man who was talking to my mother. Surprisingly, my mother seemed to be very kind to me that day. After she introduced the man to me, saying he was my uncle, she said that the man was there to take me to his village. She said he was the man who would take me to school, because I like school.

When I heard that, I became so excited and happy that I asked when we would leave; she told me that we would leave as soon as they had finish talking. On hearing that, I told my mother that I couldn't leave without breaking the good news to my close friend and saying goodbye to her. Just as I was leaving the house to see my friend, I saw my sister's baby behind our house crying. I decided to carry the baby to calm her down, not knowing that my decision to stop there out of sympathy for my sister's baby would lead to a crucial turning point in my life forever!

As I was calming my sister's baby, I overheard my mother telling the visitor, referring to me, "This is the girl I was talking about."

I vividly heard the old man's response. "As you know, when I take her, I will consider that she belongs to me. I will give lots of cows for the girl, considering she is light-skinned." As if that was not enough, he continued, "When we take her, you will never see her again because she will belong to me."

To be honest, when I heard that, I became so scared I nearly dropped dead from shock! Immediately, a thought dropped into my mind. I was reminded of a certain old man in the village who was said to visit different families when he thought there was a potential young girl that could be his wife. The old man usually gave the parents a lot of cows so that they would force their daughters to be married to him. When I overheard that plot, I decided to flee to my grandmother, who was not living far from where we used to live.

When I arrived at my grandmother's house, she was in the kitchen preparing dinner. Out of fear, I decided to go straight to the bedroom to hide, instead of greeting her. In fact, she didn't even know I was there. I knew that, if my mother didn't see me at home, the next step would be to come to my grandmother's house to ask for me. This made me even more terrified. I was aware that, if she found me in the place where I had taken refuge, she would take me by force, without needing any explanation to anyone. In the bedroom, I decided to hide under the bed to make it difficult for my mother to locate me when she decides to search for me in my grandmother's house.

Actually, it didn't take much time before my mother showed up at my grandmother's house. I overheard her asking about my whereabouts. As my grandmother didn't know that I was there, she told my mother that I was not there. Seemingly agitated, my grandmother asked my mum, "What have you done to her this time?"

My mum replied, "Nothing!" My mother complained to her that I'd told her I was going to see my friends. But when she asked my friends about me, they'd told her they hadn't seen me.

After failing to find me at my grandmother's house, my mother left, still very frustrated. It was at that time I decided to come out from my hideout to see my grandmother, who was very surprised to know that I was at her house! At that time, I was literally shaking from fear and trauma. I explained to my grandmother what had happened and my mother's secret plot against me. My grandmother told me that, as she knew my mum very well, she would not expect any less from her, as she was capable of anything. She said she would confront my mum and tell her that what she wanted to do was not right and that she disapproved.

The following morning, my grandmother went to see my mother and came back later that day with my clothes. She told me that, upon asking my mother about what she planned to do, she denied everything, claiming I was not telling the truth. However, my grandmother advised me to stay with her and promised to take me to school—as if all the odds wouldn't be in my favour.

After I had stayed with my grandmother for two weeks, she started to be ill. She became so ill that, when my uncle heard about it, he decided to come and take her to the village where he was living to take care of her.

Fortunately enough, before my uncle left with my grandmother, she told him the whole story about me, telling him that I had to go with her as well. I was so grateful that my uncle was sympathetic to my situation and decided to take me to go and live with him.

After spending some time at my uncle's house, I soon realised that, although I was safer being away from my mother, my uncle was not much better when it came to education. My uncle was one of those rural folks who thought secular education was a waste of time and was corrupt and that only religions teachings were required for children. He told my grandmother that I did not need secular education. Instead, he decided to look for a good madrasa for me so that I could get good teachings on our sacred scriptures and traditions, which would prepare me to be a descent wife when I get married in the future.

One thing I didn't understand (and don't understand to this day) is that my uncle's granddaughter, who was older than me, was living at his house. She went to school every day. But for me, nobody seemed to care about my education except my grandmother. Still, I did not care that much, as long as I knew I was safe and nobody was going to force me to get married while I was still very young.

Sadly, a few months into our stay, my grandmother got very sick, and she died. I was highly devastated upon her death. The only one who could understand me, protect me, and strive for my future education and career was gone!

In desperation, I had no choice but to go back to my mother. I went back and found that my mother was still the same alcoholic, the same person who did not care about anything but herself and money. She was always telling me she would teach me a lesson because I had refused to get married, which could have brought a lot of cows at home.

By the time I came back home from uncle's, my young brother had gone to live with my father in another region. So my mother was left with my younger sister and now me.

I met a certain lady who told me that, if I would help her with her children, she would pay me every month. I spoke to my mother, and she agreed. So I started going to the lady's house. I would start in the mornings and come back home in the evenings. Days went by, but I do not remember seeing any money from that lady. She was giving that money to my mother.

I remember my mother telling me, "I will keep and manage your money. Don't worry. Any time you want it, just tell me."

Anyway, I was too young to think about money. I knew I was working for my family, so for my mother to have my money was not a problem at all. The only problem was that, whenever she got money she would go to the *kilabuni* (pub). And after she drank, she would come home and start beating me up and threatening me, saying she would make sure I got married so that she could get lots of money.

# CHAPTER 2

## RUN TOWARDS YOUR DESTINY

Due to my mother's harsh treatment and threats, I knew it wouldn't take long for her to find me another husband. So I decided to run away to Singida town to look for a job; I'd heard people were getting jobs in Singida town. I left home secretly. Nobody knew where I was going.

When I reached Singida town, I knocked on the doors of different houses. When people came out to ask who I was, I would explain myself and tell them that I was looking for a job.

"What kind of job?" they would ask.

"Any kind of job. I am willing to do whatever you need," I would reply. And I would explain to them that I could cook, wash dishes, sweep, and fetch water.

At the first few houses I went to, I did not get anything. The people told me they did not need a maid. Then I came to the next house. When I knocked, the door was opened by a man who was extremely angry and rude. Before I had even greeted him, he asked rudely, "What do you want?"

"A job," I replied, shaking.

"What job?" he demanded.

"Any job," I replied.

"*Toka hapa! Ninyi ndio wale mnaokuja kuiba kwenye nyumba za watu*" ("Get out of here. You are one of those who come and steal from other people's houses"), he said in a very high-pitched, loud tone.

I became so scared, even to go to another house. I prayed, "God help me to get a job before it is dark."

I had no choice. I had to go to the next house, because it was evening, and it was becoming dark. I pulled myself together, and I went to another house not very far from the house of that man who had kicked me out. When I knocked on the door, a beautiful and very polite lady answered. "*Hujambo?*" ("How are you?") she greeted, even before I had greeted her.

"*Sijambo*" ("Fine"), I replied.

"What do you say?" she asked me kindly.

"I am looking for a job," I replied.

*Te-he, te-he*! She laughed and asked, "Where are you coming from?"

"*Magwa*," I replied.

She welcomed me inside; gave me some food; and, later, she told me to go and have bath. After I finished, I was shown a bedroom to sleep in. "I am sure that now you are very tired. We will talk tomorrow," she said.

"Thanks, God bless you," I said as she was leaving the room.

I slept like a person who has no problems at all, because I had never slept in a bedroom and on a mattress like that before.

In the morning, I woke up very early so that I could start working. Since it was so early, it was very quiet. I was a bit scared, but I had no choice. I wanted to impress the lady who had accepted me. So I looked around the corner, whereupon I saw a broom. I opened the door so I could go outside to sweep.

As I was sweeping, I heard someone talking behind me. "What are you doing at this time?" she asked.

"I am sweeping," I replied.

She asked, "Do you even know what time is it?"

"*Hapana*" ("No, I don't"), I replied.

"It is five in the morning!" she told me. "Go back to sleep. I will wake you up when I wake up."

I couldn't believe it. She was treating me so well. I had never experienced such good treatment before. So I went back to sleep, waiting to be awakened by her. I couldn't sleep at all. I lay there thinking of what had been happening in my life. I couldn't believe I had met a good person who had a good heart. My mind was full of thoughts.

A few minutes later, I heard someone knocking on the door. I opened the door.

"*Umeamkaje*" ("Good morning"), she said.

"*Nimeamka salama*" ("Very good morning"), I replied.

"Okay, go and finish what you started to do. And I will prepare breakfast," she said.

Immediately, I dressed and went outside to finish sweeping. By the time I'd finished, the breakfast was ready. I brushed my teeth with a stick toothbrush. Then we sat down to have breakfast.

After we'd finished breakfast, she told me about her family. She was living there with her mum and her son. But they were a way for one week. They had gone on holiday. And she told me I would stay there to help her with her son and other domestic work.

In one week's time, her mother and son came back and found me there. Though they were a bit surprised, they were happy they had found somebody to help them. I thanked

God because the lady's mum accepted me, and she was good person just like her daughter.

After about five years of living with this beautiful family, they broke very sad news to me, though to them it seemed to be good news. They told me that they wanted to relocate to another region because the son's daddy wanted to reunite with his family and live together. He'd used to come and see his family and then go back to that region where he was working. After hearing that news, I felt very bad. I had lived with that family for nearly five years.

I saw myself growing up in this family, and all these years, they had treated me so well. Basically this family had become like my true family. I begged them to take me with them. But they told me that the son's daddy already had a helper. They promised me, though, that they would help me find a job before they left. It was not a difficult moment only for me. They had to admit that leaving without me was difficult for them too; they liked me a lot. I thank God they did as they promised. They found me a new place to work.

It was 1995 and I was eleven years old when I started working at this new place for new people. It was another unexpected experience in my life. I had thought I would live with the previous family forever; they were very good people to live with. But God's plan is not our plan. We plan one thing, and He plans another.

I came to an agreement with my new employer that she would pay me 2,000 Tanzanian shillings per month.

This family had three children, two girls and one boy. I lived with the family for three years—all of which were a difficult time for me. My employer was so cruel. She used to beat me up without good reason, for example, when I broke a glass or a cup. And sometimes, when she sent me to shop, she would spit on the floor and tell me, "If this saliva dries up before you come back, I will teach you a lesson." The saliva was going to dry up no matter how quickly I went because she was spiting on sand. When I would return, inevitably to find the saliva dried up, I would be beaten severely.

Honestly, I don't know how I survived in that house for three years. Because of the way she treated me, I remember telling myself, *If she leaves her youngest child with me, she will receive the payback for all the beatings I have received from her mother.* I thank God for His voice, which was with me always. I could hear the voice telling me, "Do not do anything to this child. She is just an innocent baby who does not know what her mother is doing to you." And I remember another voice telling me, "Don't worry. These problems will not stay with you forever. This will end, and tomorrow will not be the same."

So I never touched my employer's children in any way. And I have to admit that was because of the faith I had in the voice that was assuring me; that was what prevented me from doing bad things to this family. Although I had every reason to pay her back and I knew I had the power to harm her just as she was harming me, I decided to ignore that. Instead, I loved and respected her. And I knew I had to take care of her two young children. Her firstborn was close to my age (two years older than me), so he took care of himself, though I had to wash his clothes and dishes and cook for him.

It was around five in the morning. I was busy sweeping the ground when I felt someone touch my waist. I became frightened, as it was still very dark. Full of fear, I turned around to see who was there. I couldn't believe it was James, the son of the lady I was living with. He did not care that I was shocked and scared. He wanted to touch me again inappropriately. But I didn't allow him to do that.

Every time he followed me, I ran to another side at the room. Finally he gave up, saying, "*Nita kupata tuu*" ("I will definitely get you"). And then he went back to his bedroom.

I continued working, but I was very angry and scared. I couldn't imagine what has happen. But I told myself that, when his mom woke up, I would tell her that her son had abused me.

When she woke up, I prepared her breakfast. After she had finished, I told her about what had happened in the morning, though I was so scared to tell her. I didn't know how to say it, because I was feeling very ashamed. But I told myself that I had to find a way to tell her so she could warn her son not to do that to me again. I explained to her exactly what had happened, and she told me we should wait for her son to come back from school.

Later in the evening her son came home. After dinner, she told her son to come and call me because I was in the kitchen. Immediately I realized it was time to go and talk about what happened in the morning. When James and I arrived in the living room, James's mom asked James.

"James, what did you do in the morning?" the lady asked.

"Nothing!" he replied, while looking down.

"And you, Gemma, explain here what you told me earlier," the lady asked me.

I repeated what I had told her, but he kept denying it.

"Go to sleep, my son," the lady told her son.

Surprisingly, she started slapping and hitting me. "Don't you ever speak lies about my son," the lady told me.

With pain and anger, I cried and cried. I asked myself many questions, and I even asked God why he was allowing people to hurt me so much. But the voice kept encouraging me, saying that I shouldn't give up because tomorrow would not be the same.

After this incident, I was not comfortable to continue living there anymore. The son started to humiliate and mock me. He would come to me and touch me inappropriately any how he wanted and laugh at me. He would be laughing while telling me, "If you tell my mother, you are the one who will be in trouble, just like what happened last time." He reminded me of this every time. I think he wanted to scare and to take advantage of me. Life became hard to bear; the humiliation and abuse was too much.

So I decided to leave. Besides, since I had started living with that lady, she had never paid me as we'd agreed she would when I started working at her house. She was always giving me an excuse not to pay me. She would start counting glasses or cups that I had broken and the food that I ate. Eventually she would tell me, "I don't have to pay you till you pay me back for the things that you have broken." I knew I had to leave that house as soon as possible.

But before leaving, I had to look for somewhere else to stay and work, because I knew I couldn't go back home yet.

It was evening when my employer came back home. After she had eaten, I told her that I had been waiting for her to come back home so I could go.

"Where are you going?" She asked

"I have got another job," I replied.

"What!" she said, her voice filled with shock. "Noway! You are not going anywhere. Who will take care of my baby when I go to work tomorrow?" she asked.

Anyway, eventually I left, though she begged me not to go. I was fed up with everything that was happening. I could see myself having less and less strength to carry what they were doing to me.

I started a new job with new people. I lived with this family for only about one year, as the torment and mistreatment was almost the same as at the previous house. I would cook and set the table for my employer (the lady of the house and her children) to eat. I would wait for them to eat, and then I would eat the leftovers—if there happened to be any leftovers if they had finished all the food then I would eat the burnt food —from the pot (*ukoko*). This was another difficult experience that I had to go through in my life.

For some reason the man of the house (the husband of the lady who employed me) liked me. He was always defending me every time his wife wanted to mistreat me. Unfortunately he didn't spend much time at home. He was home only Saturdays and Sundays. On these days, I will eat with them at the table. But from Monday to Friday, I would eat leftovers in the kitchen.

One day I went to fetch water. As I was returning home with the water on my head, I stepped on a stone. I fell down and broke the water basket. When I reached home without water or basket, I was severely punished for that. The man of the house was not happy about what his wife had done to me, as my whole body was swollen, especially my face and hands. When he found out what had happened, he was very angry, so he confronted his wife.

As they were taking, I heard the wife say to her husband, "Why are you so concerned with this girl? Do you want to sleep with her?"

"What did you say?" he asked his wife.

When I heard that, I felt so bad because the man was old enough to be my father. The children, who were about my age, were listening too. So I felt so uncomfortable. Besides, that man was a very respectable man in the society we were living in. He had never approached me or shown any behaviour that would lead to a sexual affair. So basically, the wife was accusing him of something he'd never tried to do to me. He was one of the people who I could call a true *Christ follower.*

He would pay me the agreed amount of money every month. For the second time, I realised that there were still good people left in this world.

Through all this difficult time, I remained a happy and joyous girl—so much so that my previous boss and the present one were asking their children, "What is wrong with Gemma? We are mistreating her, yet she is still laughing and smiling."

Even the neighbours were asking the same question. I remember one lady asked me, "Gemma, what is your secret? We all know that you are being treated unfairly, but you seem to be happy and smiling all the time." She added, "I really wish I could be like you."

As a child, I was happy, and mistreatment didn't matter that much, as long as I knew I was not going to be forced to get married. Being free from getting married to an old man kept me feeling alive. It gave me strength to patiently endure all the pain I was facing during all that time when I was on the run.

I kept telling myself, *Tomorrow will not be the same,* though this nightmare was taking a long time to end. But after my employers had argued because of me, I was no longer comfortable there. I decided I should go back home for few months while waiting for the dust to settle. I had to admit, though, that I was scared to go home. I knew if I stayed home for a long time, I might again be in danger of being forced to get married.

So I went back home, but my mind was full of thoughts. I didn't know what I was going to face when I get home.

The first three weeks, there was peace at home because I had money, which I had earned when I was working. So I had something to offer to my mom. But as the days went on, I was running out of money, and things started to turn for the worse. She would go to the pub and drink and come back home and start arguing and fighting.

After a few weeks, my cousin who was living in Singida town came to the village. He found me there and asked my mom if he could take me to town with him so that I could help his two wives with their domestic work. My mom allowed me to go to Singida town with my cousin. When I got to town, my cousin's two wives started treating me like a house girl (maid). I was not so happy living with my cousin and being treated like a person who was not related to them. My cousin had five children, and they were all going to school, but I wasn't. I had to stay at home doing all the work around the house and preparing food for them when they came back home. We used to eat off one plate, more than ten people. My cousin's first wife took advantage of my status in the home. When we were eating, she would send me to go and bring something, and when I would come back, I would find that all the food was gone.

As a young girl, I used to cry a lot because of missing food. It was such a painful moment to experience in my cousin's house. But I never mentioned anything to my cousin. I knew if I dared to say anything, I would be in trouble, especially with my cousin's first wife.

The second wife was not a bad person. She felt badly for me. But she had no power to do anything, because she was still new. According to tradition, she was not supposed to confront the first wife, no matter what.

During the time I was living with my cousin, my two elder brothers, who by that time were living in Arusha region, decided to come and take my mother to where they were living. I was left in Singida town with my cousin while my mom and younger sister were taken to live in Arusha. My younger brother was with my daddy in another region, which was very far from Singida town. There had been no communication between me and my daddy since he'd separated with my mom when I was five. So he didn't know that I had been left in Singida town with my cousin while my mom went to Arusha.

# CHAPTER 3

## LIFE IS SO UNPREDICTABLE

After a year and a half of my mother in Arusha, she remembered me. She asked my cousin to send me to Arusha, but for some reason, my cousin ignored my mom and refused to send me to join my mother.

A few months later, my brother came to Singida from Arusha. I told him what was going on in my life at that time. I explained that I was not happy living with my cousin because his first wife was treating me badly. In the evening, my brother spoke to my cousin, saying he would like to send me to Arusha. My cousin accepted my brother's proposal, and two days later, I left for Arusha.

When I reached Arusha, I lived with my mom for about two weeks. Then I had to go and live with my elder brother, who lived not far from where my mom was. I left from my mom's house to go and live with my brother, because my mom was still drinking lots, which caused her to argue and fight with me all the time.

Actually, my elder brother's wife was the one who convinced me to go and live with her after she realised how much my mom and I were fighting. My elder brother's wife was a good person. She liked me very much. I enjoyed living with her because she really cared about me. During the time I was living with my brother, a man came to the village we were living he was looking for a house girl (maid) to work for a woman who lived in a place called Kia he spoke to my mom. I was asked if I wanted to go and work in that place. Because I was already used to living away from my family, it was not difficult for me to decide to go and work for that lady. Though my sister-in-law was not happy about the idea of me living away from her, she had no choice. I had already decided to go. And I think I was happy to leave because I felt shame about what my mom was doing. So I went to Kia.

The lady in Kia was a good person. Though she wasn't paying me as we agreed, but she made sure I had food to eat, clothes, and other things I needed. The only problem I faced in that house was the lady sister's daughter, who was living with her. She was my age-mate, so when I went to their house, she was standard seven. One day, I told her that I had not been to school, so I didn't know how to read and write. I expected that she would teach me, at least to read. Instead she took advantage and started to mock and laugh at me.

One day, she and her younger sister were studying, and her younger sister asked me to help her to write something. The request was genuine, as her young sister was four years old, and she did not know that I did not know how to read and write. The older sister started to laugh, telling her younger sister, "She knows nothing. She is just a house girl. She will never know how to read and write." I felt pain in my heart.

I knew what she was saying was true. But with courage, I stood up and told her, "I will make sure one day I will know how to read and write. You just wait. You will see." I was just talking out of anger and humiliation. In truth, I didn't know for sure if I would ever know how to read and write. But for some reason, I told her that.

I have to admit it was not easy to put up with that young girl. She was so arrogant, and she humiliated me every time she got the opportunity. I couldn't believe someone could be so rude to someone who didn't know how to read and write. She called me poor and said I was a person with no significance.

One day, she dared to ask me, "Which part of Singida do you come from? Magwa. I replied. "Ooh! Now I know why you are so poor compare to us." she told me. She knew Singida very well because she was born there as well. We were coming from the same city but we were two different tribes. So she considered herself from the rich family and I was from the poor family.

I continued living with them, ignoring her attitude towards me.

In the second year of living with this family, the lady who was employing me told me I was no longer needed. Her daughter, who I had been supporting, had grown up. So she didn't need my help anymore.

Before I left I asked my employer if she would let me stay there while I looked for another place where I could go and work. I spoke with a few people, letting them know that I was looking another job. After a few days, someone came from Tengeru in search of a maid who could help his wife. I agreed with that man that would pack my stuff and he would come to take me in two day's time.

I prepared my stuff, and after two days, he was there to pick me up. On the way, he told me many good things about his family, the wife and children. The way he was talking to me, he seemed to be a good person and a gentle man.

I prayed, saying, "Thank you, God, for giving me another good family to live with."

I couldn't wait to reach my new home and meet his wife, because he spoke so highly of her. It took us one hour and half to reach Tengeru.

## CHAPTER 4

# DO THE RIGHT THINGS BECAUSE THEY ARE THE RIGHT THINGS TO DO

It was evening when we arrived in Tengeru. His wife was very happy to see me, as she was desperate to have a helper. Days went on, and the man was right about his wife. She was good person. She treated me well and with respect. She loved me like her own younger sister, which was because she had a sister who was my age-mate and who used to come to her sister when it was holiday. And so she treated me exactly as she treated her younger sister. For the first time I met a boss who would give me her own clothes to wear when we were going out, so that I would appear smart and good. I will never forget this. She would introduce me to people as her young sister, and for some reason, that was a good feeling. I felt like I was living with my biological sister.

For the first time, I felt the true love of Jesus in my life. She would mention Jesus often, but I never saw her going to church. This was because she was a Christian, brought up in a very strong Christian family, but she had decided to marry to a Muslim. Still, I could clearly see her true Christian values and beliefs in her life and in everything she said. Frankly speaking, she inspired me. She would explain to me what was in the Bible and what the Bible said about me. Listening to stories about Jesus made me feel very special, like an important person in this world. Before that I had taken myself as a person who was born to suffer in this world. After I met this woman, though by that time she was Muslim, she changed me just by giving me the stories of Jesus.

It was holiday, and her younger sister would be coming to visit. It would be the first time I would meet her, though I heard about her many times. My boss told me that her younger sister and their entire family, except her were Christians and that her young sister loved to go to church. I really wanted to go to church to see how it felt to be there. It was Friday when her younger sister came. On Saturday, I asked my boss if she would allow me to go to church with her young sister. She was very happy for some reason, and she told me, "You can go to church any time you want to go, even when my young sister is not around."

I was so excited, and looking forward to go and see what was happening. We went to church in the morning. I had to admit it was a good feeling—meeting people who were so happy to see you in church for the first time. I felt like I belonged there with them. I remember the word was preached. Though I did not know how to read a Bible, I could listen and understand what the pastor was talking about.

After the preaching was over, the pastor called for people who wanted to give their life to Jesus. Because my boss had already explained what it meant to give your life to Jesus, I could not stop myself. I felt very strongly in my heart that I should go and receive Jesus. I jumped to the front of the room, and I was prayed for. The whole church was very happy to see me receiving Jesus. I could not understand why everybody was so happy to see me there in front of the congregation receiving Jesus. Some people were crying. I did not understand why, but later I was told they were tears of joy. I was even told that, when someone gives his or her life to Jesus, the heavens celebrate as well.

When we got home, my boss's younger sister was more excited than I was. She explained to her sister what had happened to me. My boss was very happy for me.

Since then, I started walking with Jesus Christ in my life. I have to say, ever since I received Jesus, my life became meaningful, and I found a peace that I cannot explain.

As my happy life with Jesus Christ was just beginning, little did I know things were not going to be the same as I had expected in that house. Things were about to change between me and my employer (the man of the family). Although I was very happy with the life I was living there, things started to change gradually. My boss (man) started to act very weirdly. He would look at me in a way I didn't understand. He would even make a gesture as if he was kissing me. Honestly, I became incredibly uncomfortable, though I wasn't sure what exactly he wanted.

As the days went on, so too did his perplexing behaviour. One day, I was preparing a table when he came in. Suddenly, he touched my waist. I couldn't believe what had happened because he had done it without any fear, though his wife was in the kitchen while I was in the dining room. As young as I was, I decided to ignore it and pretend that nothing had happened, although I knew it was serious matter.

A few days after the incident, the lady of the house travelled to another region to see her parents, so I was left home with, Rama, the man of the house and his two children. In the evening, Rama came back from work. He called me to the sitting room, saying he wanted to talk to me about something. I went into the sitting room to listen to him. That was when I realised Rama had not been joking during that first incident. He told me that, ever since I had come to his house, he had fallen in love with me. But he had wanted to give me some time so that he could tell me that he was in love me. Honestly, I was shocked. No one had ever told me that before. I told him that, what he had told me was wrong because he was married. Rama told me marriage was not a problem. What mattered was that he was in love with me, and he was ready to marry me and make me his second wife.

While he was still talking and insisting, I decided to walk away from him. I couldn't take what he was saying any longer. I went to the kitchen. He followed me there, and he told me he would give me some time to think about what he'd said. I became very uncomfortable around him. Since I arrived to his house I had respected him. I had thought of him as my brother-in-law because I had called his wife sister.

When his wife came back, I did not tell her about what had happened. I knew telling her what had happened when she was not around could bring problems in her marriage, and I did not want that. She was a lovely lady who treated me with love and respect. I knew if I mentioned her husband's actions to her, she would feel miserable and hopeless. But I remained uncomfortable and unhappy around Rama.

# CHAPTER 5

## IF THINGS YOU DON'T HAVE CONTROL OVER GET TOUGHER, RUN!

After a while, my "employer" (the lady of the house) noticed that there was something wrong between me and her husband. The three of us used to watch TV and make stories together, but since she had come back from her village that wasn't happening any more. I tried to pretend like nothing had happened, but I couldn't do it. If I was in the sitting room when he came in, I would walk away. And when he came to the kitchen, I would walk away too. Eventually, his wife noticed that there was something wrong between us.

A few days later, she called and asked me if there was anything going on between me and her husband. Out of fear, I told her that there was nothing going on. I lied because I didn't know how she going to react towards her husband. I liked her so much, and I did not want to make her suffer because of her husband's actions. She tried to convince me to tell her what was going on. But I didn't say anything. I just kept saying, "Nothing, sister!"

Two days after Rama's wife had spoken to me about him, he came to the kitchen where I was preparing a meal.

He had the guts to ask me about the request he'd made. Basically, he was asking for an answer. I became very angry, and I shouted at him, telling him that I didn't like him and that his wife had noticed there was something going on.

"What!" he asked.

"Yes," I told him. "Your wife asked if there is anything between me and you, because nowadays I am kind of running away from you."

"What did you say?" he asked, sounding shocked.

"Nothing of course!" I told him. "But I am warning you, if you come to me with your proposals, I will tell her the truth." I answered him.

"You see, this situation is your fault," he said. "Why do you have to change your behaviour toward me so much that she realised there is something going on?" He blamed me.

I became even angrier. How did he have the nerve to tell me that, given that he was the one who had started it in the first place? Now he was telling me that it was my fault.

"Don't tell my wife anything!" he told me.

"I won't if you promise to stop," I said. "But if you continue, I will definitely tell her." Then I walked away.

Days after I had that very intensive conversation with Rama, I was mopping my bedroom. When I reached the door, something fell on me from the top of door. The item wasn't new to me; I had seen it on a TV advert—advertising what was referred to as a Salama condom. However, at that time, I didn't know the use of a condom. So I thought it was something good. I took it to Rama's wife to show her.

When I gave it to her, she was so surprised. With shock in her voice, she asked, "Where did you get this thing from?"

I told her that it had fallen from the top of the door while I was mopping.

"Are you sure it fell from your bedroom door?" she asked.

"Yes," I assured her.

"Okay. Go and continue with what you were doing," she told me.

I left there wondering why she had been shocked when she had seen me holding a condom. Nevertheless, I continued with what I had been doing.

In the evening when Rama came back from work, I heard them arguing about the condom, so I knew I had caused a problem, though I didn't know what exactly was the problem. I heard Rama's wife telling Rama that it was him who had put that condom on the top of the door. Rama continued to deny it, saying that it wasn't him.

"Rama if you are saying it wasn't you, then tell me who is responsible?" She asked him.

From there on, I didn't hear him saying anything. He couldn't answer his wife anything it seemed.

The next day, Rama followed me and asked me, "Why did you show my wife a condom?"

I didn't answer him anything because I didn't know What was going on, and I was wondering what was the big deal about Condom. So I left him without an answer.

I started to become more and more uncomfortable living in the same house with Rama, as he continued to persist in his attempt to get me to have a relationship with him. I couldn't accept his proposal because I knew it was the wrong thing to do. Rama started to tell me that I had to accept him because him and his wife were not in good terms, and I was the reason why.

"What do you mean?" I asked him.

"Why did you show my wife a condom?" he asked me.

"I only showed her because I normally see it on the TV," I answered him.

He just looked at me and shook his head as if I had disappointed him big time.

"What is a condom used for?" I asked him. I really wanted to know what its use was.

But he wasn't ready to tell me. And I couldn't ask the lady about the condom, because it was true that, after the condom issues, everything had changed. She was no longer as happy as she used to be.

"Let me marry you to show this woman" (his wife) "that I am a man!" Rama told me.

Honestly, I couldn't believe what he was saying. I just looked at him and walked away, leaving him standing there.

As the days went on, I became more and more uncomfortable. I decided to tell Rama's wife that I wanted to leave, as I was no longer comfortable living with them.

"Why is that? Have I done anything wrong?" she asked me.

"No. You haven't done anything wrong," I answered.

"Then why do you want to leave us?" she asked again.

But I just kept quiet.

"My children are used to you now. If you leave, you will hurt them so much," she said.

"Sister! I just want to go back home," I told her. And then I started to cry, because I knew she real liked me and because I liked her as well. Deep in my heart I didn't want to leave. But I had no choice. I was forced by her husband's behaviour. I couldn't take it any longer.

"'Gemma, I know there is something wrong, something you don't want to tell me," she said. "Is it about my husband?" she asked, as if she knew what I was passing through concerned her husband. She spoke to me with assurance. "Gemma, I know my husband. Just tell me what is going on."

Her words about knowing her husband convinced me, and I decided to open up to her. I explained everything that had happed from the day when she had travelled to her village.

She became very furious, and she told me, "Thanks for telling me the truth." She added, "Don't worry. All men are like this. I went for three years without a house girl because of this. I didn't want to have a maid because I did have a bad experience with the first two maids we hired. But after a few years passed, he promised he would not have an affair with another maid.

What she was saying was shocking news to me. I couldn't believe it. How could someone have been cheated on twice by her husband sleeping with the maid but still be so happy and understanding? By the time we had finished talking, she was so sad and very unhappy. I knew for sure things were not going to be the same after I had revealed the truth about Rama's behaviour towards me.

In the evening Rama came back home from work and found his wife was very angry. Even before dinner, Rama wife's asked him, "So what have you done now?"

"What do you mean?" Rama asked his wife.

"How could you approach such a little girl like Gemma?!" his wife demanded.

"What!" Rama asked, sounding shocked. "Who told you such a lie?"

"Nobody lied to me. Gemma told me, and I know what she said is not a lie," Rama's wife said.

I became so scared I didn't expect her to ask him in front of me.

Rama's face changed. It became bright red, and he

looked at me with angry eyes. But I didn't expect any less from him. I knew from that time on he was not going to be very happy with me.

Though his wife convinced me to continue living with them while ignoring her husband, it wasn't easy. Rama's hatred was so vivid. He would come home and shout at me or even call me names.

After some time, I couldn't take it any more. I tried hard to convince his wife to let me leave. Eventually she understood me and agreed that I should leave for my safety. "I don't know the next step my husband will take to make sure he gets you," she said. "So it's okay for you to leave."

She told me that she was not surprised her husband had done that to me, as he'd tried to have an affair with her biological younger sister.

A few days later, I left and went back home to Arusha. I stayed with my mom for a few weeks. In those weeks, my life was miserable. As I mentioned before, my mom was an alcoholic. This made it very difficult for me to get along with her, especially when she drank.

When I arrived back home, I explained to my mother exactly what had happened where I had been living. But all my mom told me was that I shouldn't be worried because they were so many men who wanted to marry. So I would find one who would want to marry me.

During the period of time when I was at home, someone came to the house looking for a house girl or maid. She asked me if I would like to go to Dar res salaam, which is one of the biggest cities in Tanzania. I thanked God. To me, the offer was another opportunity to get away from home. I never wanted to stay with my family for a long time. I knew that, if I did stay too long, I would be forced to get married.

# CHAPTER 6

## LIFE IN A NEW BIG CITY

I accepted that opportunity very quickly. In a few weeks' time, I travelled to Dar res salaam. In Dar res salaam, life was a bit different from other places where I had previously lived and worked. People in that city were different in terms of their thinking and ways of doing things. They viewed life in a different way. Their attitude towards life and education was different as well. So it was another opportunity for me to experience and learn new things. I was even challenged by the notion that even women took their studies at university. I couldn't believe it. The bottom line was, I wasn't going to learn much because I was still a house girl, and house girls were not treated the same as other girls. House girls or maids were considered as poor people with no wealth. Though this was not true to all the employers in Dar res salaam some few people there treated their maids or house girl with respect and in a good manner.

My life began very well with this new family. They were good people. I lived with that family for quite some time. I spent about a year and a half with them. The husband's name was Maratu, and the wife's name was Raza.

At that time, I was sixteen years old. As a teenager, I started facing the real world of adolescence. Young men started to approach me, trying to convince me to have relationship with them. But I was scared to say yes. I had a notion that having a boyfriend was a sin. So I never said yes to any relationship.

Meanwhile, I started going to church with the family, not because I wanted to go and worship but because I was supposed to go with them while they were worshiping so I would take care of the baby. While I was going to church with my bosses, I realised that I had been born again, but I wasn't baptised yet. So I spoke to the pastor. I was led in the confession prayer again, and I was baptised. After that, I became a complete born again Christian, and I was given a new name.

As a teenager, complications started. There was a young man who was a friend of the family I was living with. He gave me a certain card. I didn't know what was written on it because, as you know, I didn't know how to read. So I took the card and hid it in my wardrobe, waiting to find a person who I could trust and have read it for me. But before that could happen, Raza found out that I was hiding something in my wardrobe. I don't know how she found out, but she did.

"What are you hiding in your wardrobe?" she asked.

"Nothing," I replied.

"Why are you lying to me?" she pressed. She stood up, and then she went to her bedroom. When she returned, she was holding something in her hand. My heart was beating rapidly. I started to be very scared. I knew she had found out about my little secret.

"What is this?" she asked.

"A card," I replied.

"Take it and read it," she told me.

"I can't read," I replied.

"What?!" she shouted.

I remembered that I had once told her niece that I had been to primary school but I had stopped after standard four. That had been a big lie. I'd lied to her because she was so mean to me and she intimidated me so much. She used to call me names like: poor person, maid and some time stupid person, and she would justify it by saying: "you are a poor person that is why you are working as a maid. I had thought telling her I had been to primary school up to standard four would make my life a little better. For some reason, at that time, I thought having gone through standard four was better than not have gone to primary school at all.

"You have been to school up to standard four then why you can't read this card?" Raza asked.

I realised her niece had told her what I'd said about my school history. Since I had arrived there, I had not said anything to my employer about my past life. So she didn't know who I was or the kind of life I had passed through to be there. I became so embarrassed about the whole card thing, and now she knew that I didn't know how to read.

After the card incident, there was a very big misunderstanding. Raza started complaining about me to her friends. She told them lies about me, saying I was a bad girl and that I had bad manners and that I was still a young girl but I had boy friend. She had jumped to conclusions without knowing what exactly she was talking about. After all those complaints, I did not feel good continuing to live with her anymore. So we reached an agreement that I was not good for her and she was not good for me. We agreed that I should leave.

When I was about to leave, many families that had

admired me wished I could go to stay with them. That was because they use to say I was a good girl and a hard worker. Two days before I left, Raza told her sister-in-law, Liz, about my leaving. She told Liz that I had been good girl in the past but that I had changed because now I was involving myself with boys. In reality, I had never involved myself in any kind of relationship. That was simply because I had never wished to have a relationship. Instead, I had been running— running away from being forced into getting married.

Another issue—at least in our country; I don't know about other countries—was that, when you are a maid or house girl, you are treated as a person who doesn't have feelings, so you don't have the right to fall in love. Being a maid or house girl in Africa is the most difficult job you could ever have. Anyway, that was the only job I have ever done. I didn't know about other jobs. At least I could confidently talk about the one I had done and experienced the heaviness of it. A maid didn't have the right to enjoy freedom. Basically, when you are a maid in Africa, you become like a slave or prisoner. You work from Monday to Sunday, with no off days. You are not even allowed to keep yourself clean, as there is a notion that, if a maid or house girl keeps herself clean, she might attract her male bosses. According to many people, it's not a good idea to have a beautiful, attractive and clean maid or house girl, as by allowing that, you jeopardise your marriage.

For all my life, I had been under control of my bosses. So it was difficult to involve myself in such things. I had never had any freedom or opportunity to do anything for myself. Yet I was accused of having involved myself in relationships with boys. I do not know why Raza did what she did. We had been living okay until this thing of the card came up. So she told her sister in-law about me, saying that she couldn't take me any longer because of my behaviour and that she was taking me back to Arusha where I had come from.

Honestly, I was very scared to been taken back home. I didn't know what to expect when I get there. I begged her not to take me back home. But she didn't care about what I was asking. She had already made up her mind. I prayed hard that God would make a way for me not to be taken back home.

As they were talking, the sister in-law told Raza that she would like to try me because she need a maid. "*Niache nika mjaribishe nikimshidwa nita kujulisha tumrudishe*" ("Let me try her out. If I can't handle her, I will let you know so we can take her back), the sister in-law said.

At first Raza refused, saying that she wanted to take me back to the village as a punishment for what I had done. Her sister in-law tried to convince her, and I thank God she was successful. She eventually agreed that it was okay for me to go and live with her sister-in-law. I was so happy to hear that I wasn't going to be taken to Arusha.

Raza's sister-in-law lived a bit of a distance from Raza's house. Arrangements were made, and Liz came to pick me up a day after the agreement was reached.

On the way, Liz told me, '"I heard what you have been doing. In my house, I don't want nonsense. When we reach home, I will write all the things that I don't want you to do."

"Okay, sister," I replied. I felt like crying because I knew what she had heard about me wasn't the truth. But what do you do when you are voiceless?

Just as I was about to cry, I heard a very gentle voice inside me saying, "Don't cry. I am with you, and I will help you."

At that time, I didn't know that God was speaking to me through His word in (Joshua 1:9). I didn't even know those words existed in the Bible. During that time, I survived only with the words that came from preachers or from the born-again people who knew how to read the Bible. As you know, at that time, I wasn't yet able to read or write anything.

Starting a new job with new people was not easy. There were so many questions in my mind. I didn't know these people well. They were totally strangers to me. I didn't know what to expect from them. These people were rich and more educated, which made me more anxious and scared. On top of that, I knew that I was being taken on a trial basis. So basically my job wasn't guaranteed till they saw that I was a good girl and that I could behave. But this situation was so difficult because I didn't know how I should behave. As you know, when someone is expecting something from you, then you need to raise your standard. The thing was, I didn't know how to do that. All of this was why I was so nervous. My anxiety and nervousness didn't help. I knew life had to move on. Either I was nervous or I wasn't.

I thank God I remembered this word from the Bible (Philippians 4:6–7) that says, "Be anxious for nothing, but in everything by prayer and supplication, with thanksgiving, let your request be made known to God; and the peace of God, which surpasses all understanding, will guard your hearts and mind through Christ Jesus." The word made me be calm and helped me to stay focused. From that time on, I knew I would be able to conquer anything that comes my way. Through this scripture, I realised I didn't matter —but Christ who lives in me mattered the most. I felt energised by this scripture. The power I felt gave me more reasons to move on in life fearlessly.

It was dark and raining heavily in the evening and looked like it was 9 p.m. when we arrived at Liz's house. I was so amazed by the massive house that they owned. The house was too big, which made me feel a bit scared. I had never worked in a big house like that. I didn't know if I was going to be able to work there, simply because I didn't know where I would start working in such a massive house.

As I was waiting in the living room, I was called by a young girl who looked same age as me. "Come to the kitchen to eat," she told me.

I was given food then I had a shower. Before I went to bed, Liz told me that I shouldn't go to bed untill she speaks with me.

After I had finished eating and showering, I went back to the living room so that I could wait for my Liz to speak to me. After a few minutes, she came with a white written paper. "These are the rules and regulations for you in this house. Read them," she told me.

"I can't read," I replied.

"You're telling me you can't read?" she asked.

"Yes," I replied.

"Okay. I will read it for you," she said.

"Okay," I replied.

"First thing, don't touch my children under any circumstance. No having any relationships in my house (no boyfriend). No wearing tight clothes. Understand?" she asked.

"Yes, sister," I replied.

"I am done with you. You can go to sleep. Nyanjege will show you what you are expected to do in this house. She will be with us for a few days to give you a proper induction," she told me.

"Okay, sister," I replied.

I went to the bedroom, which was the same bedroom Nyanjege used. She was still awake.

Nyanjenge seemed to be a very happy and charming

young lady. That night, she spoke to me about the family I was about to starting living with. She told me that Liz and Asa, Liz's husband had two children. Joshua, the firstborn, was two and half years old and Merry was one year old. She told me that Liz was a good woman but, I should be very careful with Asa because he pretends to be a good person but he wasn't. She told me that Asa was a very rude man who wanted everything to be done on the spot. "If you fail that, you will be in trouble," she warned.

Nyanjenge stayed with us for one week so that she can give me induction of what to be done. In this one week, I realised that there were some days when Nyanjenge was very sad and weak. I asked her about it, but she didn't tell me what was wrong with her.

One midnight, when everybody was sleeping, I woke up. I looked on every side of the bed. Nyanjege was not there. I decided to go to the toilets. As I approach the door, I heard someone crying. I realised it was Nyanjege. I knocked on the door.

"I am finishing," she replied.

A few minutes later, she opened the door. Her eyes were very red, as if she had been crying for a long time.

"What is wrong, Nyanjenge? Why are you crying at this time?" I asked her.

"Nothing Gemma," she replied. And she went back to the bedroom.

After I had finished using the washing room, I went back and asked Nyanjege again why she had been crying.

After a long conversation, she decided to tell me what was making her so sad. She told me that she was going back home to die because she was very sick.

I asked her what she is suffering from. She just told me that she was very weak, and she knew it would not be long before she would die. The statement about dying real troubled me so much. I tried to encourage her, saying that being sick and weak didn't mean that you would die. But she seemed not to get what I was talking about. I offered her a prayer, and she accepted. I prayed for her, and it was quiet again. So we went back to sleep.

That was one day before Nyanjege was to leave us. In the morning, as usual we woke up at five in the morning to start the day. Truly, Nyanjege was very weak, and she looked very pale that morning. I thought maybe that was because she had been crying almost the whole night. She couldn't stand up for a long time. I asked myself what was wrong with her, but I didn't get an answer.

Finally the day was over, and Nyanjege left. So I was left alone. I felt so badly because I was used to her already. Knowing that she was very sick and that she was going to the village where there were no good medical services broke my heart. But there was nothing I could do to help

Before Nyanjege left she took my hand and said, "Gemma! I wish you all the best. And may your God protect you, so you don't end up like me." As Nyanjege told me that, she was crying in pain.

I really didn't understand why she was crying with so much pain, and I wondered why she was saying those things to me. I started crying as well, not knowing why I was crying to be honest. I became scared when I heard what she was telling me.

"Let's go. Let's go," Liz said.

"Goodbye, Gemma," Nyanjenge said.

"Goodbye, and God bless you," I replied.

Asa and Liz were dropping Nyanjege off at the bus station. Asa was already in the car waiting for Nyanjege and Liz. A few minutes later they left.

I was now alone as a maid in a Bungalow house, and I had to face the reality of working in that big house by myself, though there was shamba boy (houseboy) who would come every morning and leave in the evening after he had finished his work. I was not used to him, so I felt like I was completely alone.

Joshua and Merry helped me not feel too bad and lonely, as they kept me busy. Joshua and Merry were adorable children. At that time, Joshua was not attending school yet, and neither was Merry. So we spent most of time together at home. On Saturdays, Asa and Liz would be back from work in the afternoon, and on Sunday it was their day off. But the rest of the weekdays, they both worked.

Having Asa and Liz as my employers seemed to be a blessing. The first three months of living there, Asa and Liz were good to me. The two children made my life meaningful. They loved me, and they respected me, especially Joshua, who was older than Merry. Joshua was young and very mannered boy, he listened to me the same way he listened to his parents. He was an amazing child.

Liz was a wonderful woman. She had a sense of humour. She would come back home and make us laugh with her jokes. Liz cared about me just like I was her own younger sister, though she didn't have a younger sister. But she did have a younger brother. Liz treated me with love and respect. She even used to encourage me to continue to do good things. "Gemma, if you continue to live with me like this, I will do something good in your life," she would tell me. She even promised to take me somewhere where I would be taught how to read and write.

Asa and Liz were educated people. Living with them inspired me and even helped me to understand things of education more and how educated people were. Asa and Liz used to speak English to each other and to their children. So my desire to know how to read, write and how to speak English increased more and more.

When I was still there, Joshua started nursery. The school bus would come to pick him up. I very much admired the nursery teachers, who spoke English with Joshua, even though there were times when I would run from them in order to avoid the embarrassment of not knowing how to speak English.

One day, I asked Liz, "Why do Joshua's teachers never speak Swahili when they come to pick him up?"

"Because they are not allowed to speak any other language, as they want them to know English," Liz replied.

I really admired Joshua's teachers the way they were speaking English. I wished to be like them. But the truth was I would never be like them. I was just a simple maid, and most of the people who knew English were people who had attended English-medium schools. So for me to wish to be like them was impossible. English-medium schools were very expensive to attend. Only the rich people were able to take their children to those schools.

Still, in my mind, I had a small hope that one day I would be able to speak English as well. I knew there were lots of millions involved in attending those schools, yet I had small voice telling me, "One day, you will be among people who are educated and who can speak this language that you like so much."

As the days went on, I couldn't figure out how my life was going to be. I was growing up without anything tangible in my life. I started to be a little bit scared about my future life.

# CHAPTER 7

## FIGHT TO THE END: NEVER GIVE UP!

It was early in the morning, very dark, and raining heavily. That day, Liz decided she would not go to work and would instead do her work at home. Liz awoke at the same time she normally wakes up for work. She did everything she normal do when she is going to work. After breakfast, she took her laptop and went to the sitting room. She stayed there for about four hours, and then she came outside where I was playing with Merry. "Gemma, come inside. I need to talk to you," Liz told me.

"Okay, sister," I replied. I followed her behind. I was quite scared, as I didn't know what she wanted to tell me. I thought maybe I had done something that wasn't pleasing her. The way she spoke to me seemed to be a serious summons. I even looked scared.

Before she told me what she wanted to tell me, she asked, "Gemma, why do you look so scared? There is nothing wrong. I just want to talk to you," she added. "Sit down please."

I sat down, and she asked me, "How are you doing with the work and the children since Nyanjenge left?"

"Good," I replied.

"Yes, I can see that," she replied. "I have seen how you take good care of my children and how you do your work here at home. I am impressed with you, Gemma. So tell me, what do you want me to do to reward your love for my children and your hard work?"

Oh my God! I couldn't believe the compliments I was receiving from my boss. Knowing that I was supposed to tell her what I most wanted her to do for me! Frankly, I have to say I felt humbled and privileged to be asked that by my boss. Her request was like an opportunity I had been waiting for a long time. I didn't even think twice. I knew exactly what I wanted. "I want to know how to speak English like Joshua's teacher please," I said.

She became quiet for a few minutes. Finally she told me, "Okay then, although it's going to be very difficult for you since you don't know reading and writing. I will find someone who will teach you how to read and write before you start learning English. When you manage all that, I will take you to college to take a secretarial course. But I will only do that if you promise me that you will continue to behave the same and stay till Merry till she turn three years old," Liz explained.

"Okay, sister Liz. I promise I will take good care of your children, and I will stay with you till you tell me it is my time to go," I replied.

I couldn't believe what Liz had told me. Only a few days earlier, I had been wishing and dreaming to be able to speak English. Since then, I have realised that anything that you visualise or think about, you are basically attracting.

I left the sitting room so happy and knowing that my dream had started to become a reality. Knowing how to read and write had always been my dream since I was a little girl.

Having someone telling me that she would help me fulfil that long-lasting dream was very encouraging. From that moment on, I told myself I would do anything Liz tells me to do and that I would work like a slave to make sure she didn't have a reason not to do what she had promised me. I told myself that, no matter how hard that job was, I would work hard and faithfully till I saw my dream come true. I remembered the words that had come to me that day when I was in the car with Liz: "Do not cry I am with you, and I will help you." From what had just happened and the favour that I had received from Liz, I knew indeed GOD was with me, and I knew I had passed the test to stay in that house. When I had first come there, I was there on a trial basis. Now I definitely knew I would be there for a long time.

I have realised in life that nothing good comes to you without sacrifice or paying the price. When I was about to relax and start thinking that everything was now okay, little did I know that another challenge was knocking on the door in that big house.

It was around 9 p.m. one night when the electricity went off. Liz told me I should take a candle to Asa, who was in the bedroom. I took the candle to Asa. When I reached his bedroom, he told me I should put the candle on the dressing table, and I did that. Just before I stood up—I had bent over because the table was a bit low—I felt something on my back and on my chest. I couldn't believe it. It was Asa. He had come up behind me and hugged me from the behind. My whole body started shaking, as I didn't know what was happening. He didn't say anything; he was just hugging me and touching my breast, and he did all this quietly. Asa was a tall and very muscular man, and I was just a little skinny girl.

"Leave me alone!" I shouted, trying to push him away

from me. Knowing that he was doing that to me, I became so scared. I didn't know what was going to happen next. What shocked me more was that he seemed not to care that his wife was in the sitting room. I even started to think that maybe the two of them had planned to do something bad to me.

Within a few seconds, he let me go. I went straight to my bedroom because I was shaking and sweating. I knew if I went straight to the sitting room where Liz was, she would likely notice that I wasn't okay. And I wasn't sure whether or not I should I tell her what had happened. What scared me more was the fact that, all that time when Asa had been holding me, he hadn't said a word. He had just smiled like nothing was happening. He was acting like he was controlled by someone else; he wasn't himself at all. I asked myself many questions about what had just happened, but I didn't get a clear answer.

"Gemma! Gemma!" Liz called.

"Yes, sister!" I replied.

"Where have you gone?" she asked.

"I am coming," I replied.

"Where did you go?" Liz asked.

"I was in my bedroom."

"Okay. I know there is no electricity, but make sure you clear up things in the kitchen before you go to bed," Liz said.

"Okay, sister," I replied.

"Goodnight," Liz said, standing up to go to bed.

"Goodnight," I replied. I went straight to the kitchen to clean up.

While I was cleaning, just after Liz went to the bedroom, I heard someone coming to the kitchen. I thought it was Liz. But it wasn't her; it was Asa. I became scared again. I didn't know why he had come to the kitchen. He went straight to the fridge and opened it. He didn't take anything. He just stood there staring at me. "Do you know you are so beautiful?" Asa said to me.

I just looked at him with nothing to say to him.

"Goodnight darling. I love you so much!" Asa said, without a hint of shame on his face. And then he made a kiss face and left.

With fear in my heart, I finished cleaning up and went to my bedroom to sleep. But that night I couldn't sleep at all. I was so shocked about what had happened. I didn't know what was going to happen to me in the next days while I was there. I knew in my heart that I didn't want to leave. Liz had promised me that she would take me to learn how to read and write. I knew I had to do something to keep me there till I was taken to be trained. But honestly, I didn't know what I was going to do. It was a very difficult time for me. I had to decide what to do. I thought of telling Liz what was going on, but I didn't know how she would react—not to mention what his reaction would be; he was a very scary man. Something else that made me more scared of him was the fact that he owned a gun. I knew this guy was powerful—someone you shouldn't play with. I remembered what happened to me when I had reported Rama's behaviour towards me to his wife. Due to all of this, I decided to be quiet.

In the morning, I woke up early as usual, but I wasn't happy at all. Liz asked me what was wrong with me that morning, but I told her I was okay.

"You don't look okay," Liz said.

"I am okay, sister," I replied.

At that time, I realised that I was looking very sad that morning; I didn't want Liz to know what had happened last night.

A few minutes later, Asa came to the sitting room where his wife and son, Joshua, were having breakfast before they left.

Asa greeted me. "Gemma, *hujambo*?" ("Gemma, how are you?")

"*Sijambo*" ("I am fine"), I replied. I had anger inside me, but I couldn't show it to Liz.

Asa was very calm. He pretended like nothing happened. He was laughing a lot. I asked myself what was wrong with him, but I didn't get an answer. He seemed like a person who didn't have a conscience. I looked upset enough that morning that his wife had noticed. But he didn't notice anything; in fact, he seemed to be laughing at me.

"Gemma!" Liz called to me. She was still having breakfast.

"Yes, sister," I replied.

"I forgot to tell you something. Yesterday, I received news from Nyanjenge's village that Nyanjenge has passed away."

"What?!" I replied. I was so shocked by the new.

"People are spreading rumours that she died of AIDS," Liz said.

"Oh no! AIDS," I said.

"Yes,'" Liz replied, adding, "It is just rumours. She didn't have HIV, because when she came here, she didn't have such a disease. Isn't that right, Asa?" Liz looked at Asa.

"Yes," Asa replied.

But all the time while Liz was talking about Nyanjenge's death, Asa was very quiet. He even looked down, and the smile that he had been smiling disappeared.

"When she came here, we took her to a doctor. She was checked for everything, and she was okay." Liz was trying to explain to me. "So it is a lie. She never left this house by herself since she came here, so where would she have picked up the HIV?"

Asa agreed.

"People are just making up stories," Liz said again.

But I remained quiet.

*I am going back home to die.* I remembered Nyanjenge's statement when I asked her about how was she feeling. She was so sure that she was going to die, though I had told her that being sick didn't mean that you had to die. People got sick and they were healed and continued with their lives. But Nyanjenge's story was different. She knew exactly what was happening in her life. Upon hearing about her HIV, everything she told me started to make sense.

*I wish you all the best. And may your God protect you so you don't end up like me.* These were the other words Nyanjenge had said to me before she had left.

I wanted to tell Asa and Liz about the last words Nyanjege had said to me. But I couldn't. To them, the news about Nyanjege having HIV was just rumours. So I decided to keep quiet. Besides, I didn't want to talk about anything because of what had happened last night.

They finished their breakfast and left for work. Frankly speaking, I was left with so many unanswered questions about the death of Nyanjege.

After the incident with Asa, I became very uncomfortable living in that house. Every day, I was in fear; I didn't know what was going to happen to me. Asa didn't stop pursuing me. Every day that he got a chance, he humiliated me either by touching me or by looking at me inappropriately.

Asa tried convincing me by saying that, if I accepted his offer and go to bed with him, he would buy me a house, car and that he would give me the life that I deserved. "What is your problem?" he would say. "Just sleep with me, and I will make you a rich queen, and you will forget all about being a maid.

"I can't have a relationship with you because I am born-again Christian, and besides you are married. It is not good to do that to your wife," I would tell him.

"What is wrong with my wife? She will not find out unless you tell her," he would tell me.

"I can't do that," I told him over and over.

"Nobody has ever said no to me, especially a maid. So who do you think you are? You will see. I must take you to bed," Asa told me, looking at me with such an angry face.

I felt courage rise up in me, and I said to him, "Those maids and other people, they are not me. I am different. We will see about that."

He looked at me, and then he left, very angry.

I was so scared the entire time I was answering him back. But I had a bit of hope because the houseboy was outside. I knew that, if he tried to do something to me, I would scream and I would get help from the houseboy. But I also realised that, in truth, if Asa decided to do something to me, the houseboy wouldn't be able to do anything. Asa owned a gun, so I knew he could kill all of us and nothing will happen to him.

I didn't know what to do next. I was still scared to tell Liz what was going on because I didn't know how she would react. I didn't know what would become of me if I continued living there. Days went on with fear in my heart. I wished I had someone to share with, but I didn't have anyone. I was just a maid. Who would trust what I said? I just prayed to God. I remember saying, "Oh, God! Help me in this situation. I don't know what to do."

It was Monday afternoon I was in Merry's bedroom trying to get her to sleep when I heard a car horn, followed by the steps of the houseboy running towards the gate to open it. As soon as I heard the horn, my heart started beating rapidly. I knew it was Asa and Liz, but I didn't know why they had come home early that day. I never wished to see Asa around, so Saturday and Sunday were the most difficult days for me in that house. On Saturday, they would come back home around 2 p.m., and Sunday they would be at home the whole day. I was still in the bedroom when I heard steps announcing that someone was coming inside, and it seemed to be just one person. I grew even more scared, as I knew the sound of Asa's footsteps. I heard steps going to my bedroom. He opened the door without even knocking or calling my name. Little by little, I started to sweat and tremble with fear. For some reason, I felt in my heart this was the day Asa had been referring to when he had told me, "We will see about that," as no one has ever said no to him, especially a maid.

*Schritte*! *Schritte*! I heard footsteps coming towards Merry's bedroom. Immediately I stood up, because Merry was already asleep. I stood up behind the bed, and I waited for him to open the door. He opened the door as I had expected without knocking or calling me. He came into the bedroom quietly, without saying anything. His eyes were very red. I wondered why his eyes were so red. And I didn't like his quietness at all. He looked like someone who was ready for anything. He came inside and closed the door with a key.

"What are you doing?" I asked Asa.

"I want to make love with you," Asa replied.

He took his gun and car keys from his pocket and put them on the bed. He was still standing in the middle of the door. I knew that day was my end, especially after I saw the gun on the bed. I didn't know how I was going to escape this situation. It was a very bad experience. I realized my whole body was wet because of the fear when Asa came into the bedroom.

Suddenly, I saw Asa had started to take off his clothes one by one. He removed his trousers and then his shirt. So he was left with only his boxer and vest. Seeing Asa in such clothes, I felt powerless. I knew he was definitely going to rape me. I became so terrified. I had never seen any man naked before.

When he was about to take off his boxer, I shouted. Saying "Stop! What are you doing?"

"I want to make love with you!" Asa insisted with confidence, moving closer to me.

"If you take another step, I will scream!" I warned him.

"Who will hear you?" he asked me. "I have sent Juma to shop, windows and doors are closed. So it's just me and you. No one can hear you if you scream."

I realised what Asa told me was true. There was quietness outside. I knew I was in a very difficult situation. I had no one to help, except his two-year-old baby who was sleeping in the same room where he was trying to do what he was doing.

"I have been telling you I love you, but you seem not to understand my feeling towards you; I want to show you how much I love you." Asa said.

"What kind of love is this?" I asked him, while deep inside, I was terribly frightened. I knew that, even if I screamed, no one would hear me as he had said. I was all alone, and I really needed help.

As he was coming closer and closer to me, I remembered something. I opened my mouth, and I said to him, "If you dare touch me and have sex with me, I will surely die at your hands. So please, I beg you. Do not do what you want to do to me."

He looked at me with shock. "Why are you saying you will die if you have sex with me?"

"A few years ago, I made a covenant with God that I would never have sex or an affair with a married man," I answered him.

"Well good then! Let's have sex, and when you die, we will die together because I love you," Asa said to me.

I begged him not to rape me, but he seemed not to care about anything I said.

As we were talking about the covenant that I had made with God, he quickly took off his boxer. And he was naked before me. When I saw that, I knew this person was serious. No matter what I said, he had already made up his mind to have sex with me.

*Oh, God! Help me and don't let me sin against you with this man! Remember the covenant I made with you. Don't let this man rape me.* I prayed that prayer silently. "Get out of this bedroom," I said to him confidently.

"Ha ha haaa!" Asa laughed. "There is no way I am leaving this room without having sex with you." He said again, "No woman has seen my nakedness and leave without having sex with me, that's is not going to start with you."

"Who told you to come here and start taking off your clothes?" I asked him with confidence.

"This is my house. I decide what to do and where to go. You don't tell me what to do. You are just a maid here. Don't forget that," Asa replied.

All this time when we were talking, he was still standing in the middle of the room, blocking the door so that I would not have a chance to escape. After the silent prayer that I prayed, I started to feel very confident and strong. I felt like

I was stronger than him. I felt like I was able to do anything to Asa without him doing anything to me. All fear was gone.

As I was looking at him, I heard a very clear voice say, *Go and push him away from the door.*

Immediately, another strong voice argued, *Don't dare do that. He will kill you. He is stronger than you. Just sleep with him. There is no problem.* That voice was very strong, and it nearly convinced me that I was powerless and that I couldn't fight him; because he was a man, I should just accept him.

I fought so much with those two voices. It was true. By looking at us physically, I was very weak compare to him. I was a little girl and very skinny; fighting with such a tall and muscular man didn't add up. And looking at the gun there on the bed, I was even more confused.

I decided to follow the first silent voice, because I believed that, if he managed to rape me, I would die anyway. I decided it was better to try to rescue myself. If he killed me, it would be better than having him rape me. I couldn't see the future after he raped me. It was so hard for me to see myself after being raped by someone who was married to a person who had been so kind to me. As I stood staring at him, I tried to figure out how I would push him. Suddenly I felt like someone was trying to push my legs towards Asa.

As I moved closer to him, he came towards me faster. He held my two hands and started to push me towards the bed where the baby was sleeping. As he was pushing me, I pushed him back. As a result, he fell on the bed like a piece of paper. At the time, I didn't know where I had gotten that strength from, but now I know it was God who gave me that power and the courage to face such a giant man. When he fell on the bed, I opened the door and started to walk down the long corridor that led outside. As I was walking, I felt that I should go back and warn him.

"Don't do that to me again. If you dare do that, I will tell your wife," I told him.

Asa kept quiet. He seemed to be in shock. I was in shock as well. I couldn't believe I had actually escaped that cold-hearted man. I went outside to see if the houseboy was back, but he was not there yet. I decide to stay outside to wait for the houseboy, I was very scared. I wanted to run away, but I didn't know where I would go. I knew Asa might follow me with a gun and kill me before I could tell his wife what had happened. I was so terrified with the whole thing. I had never felt such a fear in my life.

"Gemma!" Asa called. "Come and take the baby.

"Bring her here," I replied. I didn't want to give him a chance to humiliate and abuse me again.

He brought the baby outside. She was crying because we had woken her up when Asa fell on the bed. The baby was very unhappy.

I waited and waited for the houseboy to come back, but he didn't come back that day. Instead, he came the next morning.

A few minutes after Asa had given the baby to me when I was still calming her down, Asa came outside. He didn't say anything. He just got into the car and left. I felt a little bit of relief, though I was still shaking.

It was around seven in the evening when I heard the car horn at the gate. My heart started beating wildly because I knew it was Asa. I went immediately to open the gate. I was right. It was Asa, and Liz was with him.

I greeted Liz and went inside to prepare the table for them to eat. All this time, Asa was talking to his wife as if nothing happened. I real felt sorry for Liz because she didn't know what was happening within her own house.

It wasn't easy to live in one house with a man who had

tried to rape me, but I also really wanted to know how to read and write, and Liz was the only person who had ever promised to fulfil that long waited dream. I didn't want to complicate things between Asa and Liz. I knew if I tell Liz what had happened, things might go badly for me and in their marriage. I didn't know how Liz would react to what had taken place between me and her husband. I was really scared about what was going on in that house.

Ever since the incident with Asa, I started to have nightmares—all about Asa. Every time I dreamed about Asa, he would be either killing me or raping me.

# CHAPTER 8

## PROTECT YOUR DIGNITY NO MATTER WHO YOU ARE

About a week after the incident with Asa, he came to the kitchen where I was preparing food and said to me, "Gemma, I want to apologise for what happened between us a few days ago."

"Apologise?!" I replied, shocked. I couldn't believe that Asa was actually apologising to me.

"Yes, Gemma. I am serious. Forgive me for treating you in such a bad manner; and thank you for not telling my wife." Asa's apology seemed to be genuine, but I didn't trust him at all.

"I have forgiven you since the day you did that, and that's why I didn't tell your wife," I replied.

"Gemma!" Asa called to me. "I would like to ask you something."

"What is it?" I asked. "Where did you get the strength to push me that day? I am still wondering what exactly happened. You pushed me, and I fell on the bed like a piece of paper."

I just kept quiet.

"You Chaga people are very strong," Asa said. Asa thought I was Chaga, the people from Kilimanjaro.

"That strength was from God!" I answered Asa.

"Oh! Now I know your God is very strong," Asa said, laughing.

"Yes, my God is strong," I assured him. "He will not let anyone take advantage of me.

"Okay then," Asa said, adding, "Don't be scared of me anymore please. I don't want my wife to notice anything."

"That will depend on you whether you don't repeat what you did to me. Your wife will never find out what you did but only if you treat me with respect," I warned Asa.

He smiled and left.

I didn't know if Asa was really serious about the apology. The way he was apologising and the way he was talking didn't seem serious or sincere. He was laughing and smiling without any reason when he was talking so I knew it was just a matter of time before he comes back with his nonsense again. But I just kept my faith high, believing that nothing bad was going to happen to me.

Since I had managed to push Asa in such a way, my faith became stronger. I knew that I was protected by God.

There is a Swahili proverb that says, "*Ng'ombe wa masikini hazai*" ("The cow of the poor person does not give birth"). As the days went on and on, one day I was in the kitchen cooking when I heard Liz calling me.

I went to listen what she was saying.

"Sit down. There is something I need to talk to you about," Liz said.

I sat down.

She opened up by saying, "Since you started living with me, I have not had any problem with you. I have not seen you doing anything that other teenagers do. You have lived with me with respect, and I think you deserve to have your own family." After Liz had told me that, she continued by saying, "My brother-in-law's younger brother is looking for a good wife, and I think you could be the type of wife he is looking for." She didn't stop there. "You would make a good couple because you are a born-again Christian, and he is a born-again Christian as well. So don't worry about anything. Besides, you are now grown up. For how long are you going to work as a maid? It's better to have your own house instead of jumping from one house to another."

All this time, I didn't answer anything. I was just quiet. I thought for a few minutes, and I realised that Liz had a point. It was my time to move on with my life and have my own house. Deep inside my heart, I knew if I kept living in other people's houses, I would continue to face what I had just recently faced in Liz's house. I was sixteen years old at that time, but it didn't matter that much to me, because at that point, I knew I should forget about learning how to read and write. The way Liz was talking about this matter suggested to me that was the case, she was convincing me more than giving me an option. "How about me leaning to read and write and the course you promised me?" I asked Liz, just to hear her opinion.

"Don't worry about that. I have spoken to the person who wants to marry you. He knows everything about you," Liz answered. "He is an educated man. He will definitely take you to school. I am sure he will want you to learn at least how to read and write.

I asked Liz. "Can you please talk to him about the plan that we had when your child grows up?" I wanted her to share my plan with the person who was interested in marring me. "Yes. I will tell him about what I promised you and what you really want," Liz replied.

The man was tall and good-looking. That was my judgement when I saw his picture. I didn't know much about him because I had never met him. So I had to accept him just by looking at his picture. So without hesitation, I asked Liz, "Did you say he is a born-again Christian?"

"Yes," Liz answered.

After the answer I got from Liz, I convinced myself that this man was what I asked God for. I used to pray that, when I reached the time to get married, I would meet a person who loved my God. So when I heard about this gentleman, I knew it was a time for me to get married. Without any doubt in my heart, I accepted, saying that I would get married to the person I had just seen on the photo.

Liz became very happy when I said yes to what she had proposed.

A day after I accepted the person, Liz sent a photographer to take my photo so that she could send it to the person who wanted to marry me. I had my photo taken, and a few days later, the photo was sent to the man. It didn't take long for that person to accept me as well, just by looking at my photo.

Liz became very happy. But there was someone who wasn't very happy with the idea. That was Liz's husband. After I had accepted this man, Asa came to me again. He said to me, "Gemma, please can I test you before you get married? I have never tested a virgin girl before."

"What?!" I shouted at Asa. "How can you say that to me? I am about to get married and you want to sleep with me?" Tears were pouring from my eyes. I couldn't believe someone could be so evil. I felt dishonoured and valueless. "You are cold-hearted man!" I told Asa while breaking with tears. "You recently asked for forgiveness, so you didn't mean it, I guess?"

"Oh! I am sorry again. I was just trying my luck. I

thought you might accept me because you are soon going to get married. You have nothing to lose anyway." Asa said that to me without shame on his face.

"You are wrong. No one will touch me except the person who will marry me," I answered Asa.

"Don't be so selfish. The Bible says that we must not deprive each other," Asa said quoting 1 Corinthians 7:5 in an effort to convince me that I should accept him.

I was so disappointed in him. How could he use God's word to justify his evildoing? I walked away from Asa because I knew, if I continued talking to him, we would not finish the conversation. He seemed determined to have sexual intercourse with me before I got married. I honestly didn't understand why this man never wanted to give up. He continued trying to convince me and to seduce me, but he never got what he wanted from me.

It was about a week after the gentleman had seen my photo when he said that he wanted to marry me as soon as possible. We didn't have much time to prepare. I remember Liz telling me, "I agreed with the gentleman. The sooner you guys marry each other, the faster you can start a new life together. Why wait if you are both born again and you seem to like each other?" Liz based what she was saying on my decision and the gentleman's reactions to the photos we had exchanged and the fact that the gentleman didn't want to wait for a long time.

I had to plan to go to Arusha to give my family the news. Though I wasn't so sure about getting married, I thought it was a good thing to do and that I had to pretend I wanted to get married and I was ready for that. I travelled to Arusha because we were running out of time according to the gentleman and Liz.

# CHAPTER 9

## DON'T BE DISAPPOINTED WHEN THINGS GO THE WAY YOU DIDN'T EXPECT

I arrived in Arusha around 5 pm.My family were very happy to see me after a long time. I thank God that when I went to Arusha, my father had arrived three days ahead of me. He had been living in Singida since he and my mother had separated, while my mother was in Arusha living with my elder brothers. I was so happy to see my father, and he was happy as well. Before we went to bed, I told them what had brought me there. My father seemed not very happy when I told him that I wanted to get married, which was the opposite reaction I had received from my mother. She was happy for me to get married. Deep inside, I knew she was happy because she knew, if I get married, I would be able to help them. My job as a house girl wasn't helping them that much.

"Okay. Go and rest now. We will talk tomorrow," my father said to me.

My father is a very wise man. I knew he had something on his mind that he didn't want to tell me at that time.

In the morning after we had our breakfast, my daddy called me. "mama."

"Yes, Daddy!" I answered.

"Why do you want to get married now?" he asked.

For a few minutes, I kept quiet because I didn't have a clear answer. "Daddy, I have been away from home for so many years, and all this time, I have been a maid. The things I have experienced all this time in people's houses I think it is enough. It has to end now. Besides, Daddy," I added, "if I say I don't want to get married, where will I go to live?"

He looked at me without an answer. "Okay, Mama! If you are sure this is what you really want, then go ahead. I am blessing you. May God give you happiness and joy in your life, and may He give you beautiful children like you." As my daddy blessed me, I could see tears coming from his eyes and because of that I found myself crying as well.

I had mixed emotions. I had found my father in Arusha after so many years of separation and now he was there to bless me to get married. I truly felt good about seeing him after so many years. On the other side I felt bad because I knew that, deep inside he didn't want me to get married. But he didn't have a choice. He had to let me go ahead with my plan.

After two days my elder sister Asia also came to visit from Kenya. My sister and I talked a lot about life. I shared with her about the kind of life that I have been living all this time when she was away. My sister left home when I was still a young girl, and we have never met till this time. She used to come back home, but because I was not around at home, she never knew what happened in my life, and I never knew what her experiences in life were.

So for me, this opportunity to speak with my sister face-to-face was a crucial moment and amazing experience.

I explained to her what had happened to me in all the years when she was away.

After I had finished telling her about my experiences in life, she started crying. This was what she said: "Oh! my young sister, why has life been so unfair to us this way!"

When I heard that statement, I started crying as well. I realised she hadn't been very happy in her life either. Although she never told me what she had experienced, her statement made me to understand she had bad experiences as well.

"Sister, I forgot to tell you something else," I told Asia.

"What is it?" she asked.

"There is someone who wants to marry me. So I have come to bring the news to Mother and Father."

Asia looked at me, and she took a deep breath. "What did you say?" Asia asked, as if she didn't hear what I said.

"There is someone who wants to marry me," I replied.

"How old are you?" Asia asked.

"Seventeen years old," I replied.

"Are you sure you are ready to get married?" Asia asked.

"There is nothing that I am waiting for, what else is better than getting married," I replied.

"Where is this man from?" Asia was asking what tribe my future husband came from.

"He is from Musoma, and he is from kuria tribe," I replied.

"What? You are not serious," Asia said. "Do you know this tribe?"

"No," I replied.

"Don't even think about getting married to those people. Don't you know the kuria people beat their wives to death?"

"No. I don't know that. But even if they do that, this

man will not do that to me, because he is a born-again Christian." I told my sister.

"What is being born again? Culture is just culture," my sister said to me.

I could see that she wasn't happy at all with the idea of me marring such a man from that tribe. "Sister, there is nothing I can do," I told her. "You know that I can't stay here, and I can't continue living in people's houses because of what I have been experiencing. I can't afford to be risking my life anymore." At that time, I couldn't imagine myself living with people again as a house girl. But at the same time, when I thought about what my sister had said about this tribe, I became a bit scared. I didn't know what to do. I just became quiet, looking at my sister even though I knew she didn't have any solution for my problem.

"You know what! I have an idea," my sister said.

"What idea?" I asked.

"I am not going back to Kenya. Why don't you live with me till you get the right man to marry you," Asia said to me.

And for a moment, I thought that was good idea.

While I was trying to think, my sister said, "There is nothing to think about. I am not going to tell you to go and get married to that man, because I know what I'm talking about. So you are not going back to Dar es salaam and remove the idea of getting married now."

When I heard my sister saying she was ready to live with me and that she wasn't going back to Kenya, I felt good and relieved. Still, I didn't know how long that feeling was going to last; every time I saw hope in my life, I knew there must be disappointments in the end.

At that point, there was no way I was going back to Dar es salaam to continue with the marriage issue. My sister rented a house in Kia, where I had lived before and which was not very far from where our mother was living. I started living with her there.

I had to admit the idea of me not going back to Dar res salaam to get married made my Daddy very happy. A few days later, he went back to Singida, where he was living with my other brother.

My sister and I continued to live in Kia. Later, my sister met a certain man who I had known long before. This guy wanted to have a relationship with my sister. But I was not very happy with that idea. I had once lived with a lady whose young sister had a relationship with the man. After many years of their relationship, the young sister of that lady who at the time was my employer died. When she was very sick, she had come to live with her sister. Since I was the maid there, I had taken care of her. So I had seen how she suffered till her last breath. I had heard rumours that she died because she had AIDS. This was why I did not approve of Asia having a relationship with that man. I even explained to her why she should not accept the man. But I guess what I was saying wasn't adding up because the man was so handsome and looked very health. Nobody could believe that such a strong and healthy man had HIV.

Asia was among those people who didn't believe that the man might have HIV, despite what I told her. My sister went on and married that man, and they started their new life together. I continued living with my sister and my brother-in-law. All the time I had been there living with my sister I had no other plan than the one we had made together. The only thing in my mind (and in my Asia's mind as well) was that I should stay there with her until the right man came to marry me.

Living with my sister wasn't bad at all. The only thing that bothered me was the fact that I was living without something that interested me—something that made me want to wake up and do. It was such a tasteless life. At that point, I learned that living without purpose, hope, and plans for your future is as if you have completely stopped living.

It was around five one evening when I came back home from my friend's house. I found my sister and brother-in-law waiting to talk to me, and they seemed very happy and excited. "Gemma! Please come in," my sister called me.

"Yes, sister," I responded.

"Sit down," Asia said. "Your brother-in-law has something to tell you.

"There is a man I know very well who is interested in you. He wants to marry you," my brother in-law said.

"What?!" I said, in shock. "Who is this man? Do I know him?" I asked.

"Yes you know him well." My brother-in-law told me who he was talking about.

It was true that I knew the man, but I never would have expected him to have interest in me. He was a good-looking guy, tall and very handsome. But at that point, I had certain standards for the man I wanted. And that was simple—the man I would marry had to be a born-again Christian.

Unfortunately or fortunately, the man my brother-in-law was referring to wasn't a born-again Christian. In fact, he was Muslim. So I refused straight away.

Asia and her husband were not very happy when I refused. But I knew one thing; my sister wasn't going to force me to get married to that man.

"Gemma!" my sister protested. "We women don't have religion or denomination; you can get married to any man you want regardless of his religion or denomination. Look at me," she added. "I am Muslim, but I'm married to a

Christian." My sister continued to try to persuade me to accept the man.

"No, sister," I told her. "I am not going back to where I have come from." What I meant was I was once a Muslim, and I was not going back to be a Muslim again.

"It's up to you. I can't force you to do what you don't want to do," Asia finally said. "It's your life. You can continue to wait for your born-again Christian."

Time went on and on, and life continued. But as the days went on, things started to change little by little between my sister and my brother-in-law. Suddenly they went from being people who loved each other to arguing and even sometimes fighting. Honestly, the situation made me very uncomfortable. I started to think of leaving again and once again being a maid. At first I thought maybe they were fighting because of me continuing to live there with them. But my sister assured me that wasn't true and that I wasn't the cause of their fighting. I was a bit relieved to know that I was not the one bringing the problems between them. Yet I really wished not to see my sister stressed and as unhappy as she was.

One day, they argued and fought till my sister went to get a knife. She wanted to stab her husband. That day, I became very unhappy and angry. I couldn't sleep well that night because the picture of my sister carrying a knife wouldn't leave my mind.

In the morning, I decided to talk to my sister about what had happened the previous night, as what she had done was really bad. "Sister, what were you thinking yesterday when you wanted to stab your husband?" I asked Asia.

She looked at me and kept quiet.

"Sister, why there is no peace between you anymore?" I pressed.

"You are still very young. If I tell you now, you won't understand what I mean," Asia answered while tears streamed down her face.

I couldn't stop myself from crying as well. "Sister, what is eating you so much this way?" I asked. My sister seemed to be in so much pain.

She wanted to tell me, but she couldn't open her lips to speak. After few minutes, she repeated what she had said to me. "You are still young, Gemma. If I tell you what I am going through, you won't understand what I mean."

"Is this how marriage is?" I asked.

"No, Gemma!" Asia said. "Marriage is good, but it has some challenges, like what your brother-in-law and I are passing through. And what you see here doesn't mean that you will experience the same challenges." She added, "One day I will tell what is troubling me. But if I don't have a chance to speak to you about it, Mom will tell you. She knows what is going on between me and your brother-in-law. It hurts so much to know someone has decided to kill you purposely without any reason. The pain that I feel is eating me alive. Asia said.

"Anyway, enough of this talking go and fetch water. There is something else I need to talk to you about, but it will have to wait till evening because now we have to do other things."

I left, heading to the place where we fetched water. On the way, I kept asking myself what my sister wanted to talk to me about.

It was already evening when I came back from fetching water. I prepared dinner, and while we were eating my sister told me what she had to say. "There is doctor whose name is Kimatari. She has a friend who is living in a place called Boma, which isn't very far from where we are living.

Dr Kimatari's friend has a sister who is living in Dar es salaam." Asia explained that, the woman has a daughter who is living abroad. "She needs a maid, as she is very busy with her studies," my sister explained. "And above all, she is expecting. The doctor thinks you are the best candidate for that job."

When my sister finished speaking, my heart was filled with joy and happiness. I actually could hardly believe what my sister was saying. The country that she had mentioned was one of the great European country—a country everyone in Africa, rich and poor dreams to go.

"Before anything else, the doctor need to see you," Asia said.

After a long talk with my sister, I went to bed. But I couldn't sleep. I was overwhelmed by the fact that I would be going abroad.

In the morning, I went to the doctor's house to hear what she wanted to tell me. The doctor told me that she had observed me since I had come to live with my sister. In addition, she had been asking people about me, and she had received very positive recommendations about me. Therefore, she was very convinced that I was the right person for what her sister's friend was looking for. She said that I should go with her to a place called Boma to meet her friend. I asked her if the people I was going to live with were good people. She was honest with me. She told me that she didn't know the people I would be going to live with, but she just knew her friend, who was a very good person.

We went to Boma and met her friend. She was very happy to see me, and she asked me if I had gone to school. Frankly, as I was ashamed, I lied. I told her that I had done primary school. That was a big lie, and I had to tell it because

I wasn't ready again to let anyone know that I didn't know how to read or write.

As we were talking, she gave me a certain document that she wanted me to sign. Honestly, my hands started to sweat. I couldn't hold the pen properly, as I had no idea how to do that, especially in front of educated people like them.

"Gemma, have you real been in school?" Dr Kimatari's friend asked.

I kept quiet.

"Don't worry. Even if you haven't been to school, it doesn't matter," the doctor's friend said, clearly noticing I was having difficulties signing.

On the way back home with Dr Kimatari, I barely spoke because I had so many questions ringing in my mind. I asked myself, *What if they want someone who is Educated? What if I manage to go abroad? Will I be able to communicate with people there?*

"Gemma what are you thinking?" the Doctor asked.

"Nothing," I replied.

"Don't worry. Before you leave, I will give you my contact information. If you encounter any problem that needs attention, don't hesitate to call me, and I will know what to do," the doctor said.

For a minute I felt assured that I was definitely going to Dar res salaam to start the process of my departure to Europe. The plan was to go to let my mother know that I was planning to go abroad and to put my stuff in order. I was ready to go to Dar res salaam, which was supposed to happen as soon as possible.

# CHAPTER 10

## WHEN DESTINY CALLS

I went to my mother and explained to her about my visit. She was very happy to know that I was going to Europe. The following day, I went back to Asia, who was now not feeling well. I did not know what was wrong with her, but the night before I was to leave, she blessed me. "Gemma, when you come back, I will not be around. That is certain. But what I am asking you is that you continue to be good girl. Take good care of our mother regardless of what she has done wrong. And be very careful about every man who comes in your life, because nowadays, there are so many diseases."

This made me wonder what was bothering my sister. I cried a lot as she was talking to me. This was my first time being given words of wisdom about life. It was especially poignant that those words were coming from my sister, who I knew was in pain, though she was trying to talk as if she was okay. I could see in her eyes that she was in pain. I asked her where she would be when I came back—what she had meant when she'd said she wouldn't be around.

She responded, "Gemma, never mind for now. You will find out when the right time comes."

After Asia and I had finished talking, I went to bed ready, for the journey the next day. I had a sleepless night, as I was thinking about so many things. First, why was my sister talking as if she was going to die? And what if people who were going to do my process in Dar res salaam found out that I did not know how to read and write? I thought about this question over and over again, but I did not have the answer.

In the middle of these thoughts, I had a flashback about dreaming of going to Europe when I was about seven years old. I'd had this dream especially whenever I had seen plane passing in the sky. This gave me hope that maybe now it was time for that dream to be reality, and this thought washed away my worries.

Around 5 a.m., I woke up and started preparing for the journey. I packed everything I wanted, and my sister woke up around 6 a.m. to help me finish packing and preparing breakfast. After getting everything ready, I had breakfast. Then my sister and my brother-in-law escorted me to the bus station.

I took a bus from Kia to Boma to meet Dr Kimatari's friend, who was supposed to give me a bus fare and all the other things I would need for the rest of the journey to Dar res salaam.

I reached Boma around 10 a.m. But I could not take a bus to Dar res salaam straight away, because the person I was supposed to meet was already at work. She told me that I couldn't go to Dar res salaam that same day and that I should wait until the following day when she would be able to process the ticket and everything early. She took me to her house, and then she went back to work. She didn't live very far from her workplace. I spent the whole day there with her two cute boys, who were very well mannered and disciplined. They enjoyed my company on that day, to the point that they didn't want me to leave the next morning; they were crying at the thought of my departure.

Eventually I left. That wonderful lady took me to the bus station, and she made sure that I was on the bus. She gave me some money to use while I was travelling and all the contacts I would need when I had reached Dar res salaam.

I reached Dar res salaam around 5 p.m. Since I didn't have a mobile phone, I went to a place where I had to pay for a phone call. I called my host and waited to be picked up at the bus station. While I was waiting, I was worried, as the people who were coming to pick me up didn't know me and were to identify me by the colour of my clothes.

After a while, I saw two people, a man and a woman. I walked towards them and asked them if they were the ones who were coming to pick me up.

Before they answered my question, the lady asked me, "What is your name?"

"Gemma," I answered.

"Yes we are the ones," she said.

They introduced themselves to me, and at that point, I felt at ease. I had found my host.

We rushed to where they had parked the car, and the lady started to drive. They were so charming. On the way, they chatted with me, which made me to feel welcomed and comfortable. When we reached their house, I was introduced to the family members who were around. Then later, after dinner, I went to sleep.

In the morning, I met the woman whose daughter I would be going to live with abroad. She seemed surprised when she saw me, as I looked very young. She asked me, "Will you be able to work? How old are you?"

I told her my age and reassured her that I would be able to work, as I had been working all my life since the age of seven.

She was impressed with my answers and told me, "We will soon start the process for your passport application." This was necessary, as I didn't have a passport.

After I had been there for a few days, my hosts started to process documents so that I could apply for a passport. As I was applying for my passport, some challenges started unfolding. I was asked to fill in a certain form. Instead of do so, I started shaking and my hands started sweating.

"What is wrong with you?" the woman asked.

At first, I stayed silent, but then I told her that I didn't know why I couldn't write.

Luckily, she didn't continue with that conversation. "Bring the documents to me," the lady said.

I gave them to her, and she filled in the form and then handed it back to me. "Please sign it," she said.

I quickly remembered that I had once learned how to write my signature. Among the houses I had worked in, there was a girl who had taught me and explained to me what a signature was and how to write mine. From that time on, I had memorised all the letters in my name. Little had I known how handy that lesson would become in the future. At that point, I realised that there was God who could see our future and prepare us to be able to face it without fear or surprise. I managed to sign the documents, and we dropped them off at the appropriate office.

A few days later, we got all the documents we needed for processing the passport. We didn't waste any time. We applied for my passport, and in one week's time, I got the passport.

Frankly, I felt as if I had the whole world in my hands. All the dreams I had—dreams that had seemed to be dying— were coming alive again in me. The dream of changing my life and my family's lives seemed so real. I felt so good and happy. Even my hope and faith increased. I was sure now that I was going to Europe.

While I was waiting to apply for a visa, the lady who was helping me with the process came to me and said she wanted to talk to me. "Gemma , there is a change of plan," she said. "You are not going to Europe anymore."

I kept quiet for a moment because I couldn't believe what she was saying. "Oh okay. So I have to go back to Arusha?" I asked her, shocked.

"Gemma , just take your time. You don't have to go now," the lady answered.

At that point, I felt like someone had ripped my heart and dreams completely. All the happiness I had turned into pain and sorrow. I knew nothing good would ever come to me, because every time I had hope and faith about something good, it ended badly. I started to ask myself what I had done to deserve such misfortune in my life. I even started to question if God really existed.

In the middle of all this and with so many unanswered questions, the mother of the woman who I was going to live with in Europe came to me. "My daughter has decided to bring my grandson home," she explained. "That's why you are not going anymore. But my grandson will need someone to take care of him, as my daughter is going back to Europe to finish her studies. I think you are the best person to take care of my grandson."

While I was there waiting for the baby to come, I learned many things. I was surrounded by educated people. I found myself getting interest in learning things. One thing I will never forget learning while I was in that house was how to read a clock. I used to ask people what time it was. After getting the answer, I would run to the wall clock to see what that time looked like. I continued doing that for many days, and eventually I found that I could read the clock myself. That to me was the greatest achievement I could ever achieve. The joy and peace I felt when I realised I could read a clock, no one can explain. I felt like I had been set free from the trouble I'd had of not knowing how to read a clock.

The days went on and on, and finally the baby arrived. But before I started taking care of the baby, we had to sit down and agree how much they were going to pay me. "How much do you want us to pay you?" the grandmother asked.

I didn't want to be paid every month. I was thirsty to go to school. "Just keep it for me. When the baby grows up, you will pay me so I can go to college," I told the grandmother.

She looked at me and said, "If you take care of my grandson well, I promise you I will take you to school where you will do Form 1 to Form 4," (which would mean completing my O levels).

In the back of my mind, I knew going to O level would be impossible. I just knew that, when the time came, I would take the money that she would give me (I didn't know how much that would be) so that I could go to any place where I would be taught how to read, to write, and to speak English. At the time, that was the only desire I had in my heart.

Even thought she had promised to take me to secondary school, I still wasn't ready to reveal to anyone my school background. Past experiences taught me that, once I tell my employers that I had never been to primary school, they would start to humiliate and mock me. This was what other people I have lived with before, especially the children had done. Deep inside my heart, I knew that my newest employer would not fulfil her promises, just as had been the case with other people I had lived with before. You do your part but when it comes a time for them to do their part, it becomes a problem. So I told myself that I was not going to lift my hopes up again. I would wait and see what the future would bring when the baby grew up.

I agreed with the grandmother, and the baby was brought. He was a few months old when he came, and by that time I was seventeen years old. So it was a bit challenging to take care of a little baby. Though I'd had experience with babies, this was a bit different. With this baby, it was like he was my baby. We slept together, woke up together, and spent our day together. He was by my side all the time. I had to learn the hard way to know when he was okay and when he was sick. He became like my own child. I got so attached to him and he to me. I never wanted to hear him crying or to have anybody messing with him. Life was challenging, but that boy brought joy and happiness to my life. I found the meaning of life in that boy. I became so excited about life, looking forward to wake up every morning to serve a child; that gave me fulfilment.

There was another little girl who I was kind of taking care of as well. But she was much older than the baby who was my primary charge. She was already in primary school when I arrived at the house. I admired her because she spoke English, and she could read and write as well. I really wished I had been able to do what she was able to do at her young age. Little by little, I started to get interested in knowing the alphabet. I could go where she was doing her homework, and I started to ask her questions.

One day, she was singing about the alphabet. I asked her, "What are you singing?"

"The alphabet song," she answered.

"Can you please start from the beginning?" I asked her in a way that would keep her from finding out that I didn't know how to read.

She started saying and writing all the letters of the alphabet. When she finished, I asked her for the paper she was writing on. She gave it to me, and I knew that paper would help me to learn.

Whenever she told me a letter of the alphabet, I never forgot it. I would memorise it and try to keep it in my head. As the days went on, I started to know a few of the letters of the alphabet, which I had learned from the young girl. She even used to ask me to help her with her homework, because she believed that I was able to help her. Little did she know, I didn't know anything. Every time she asked me to help her, I would ask her questions first. For example, I would ask her to write "ABCD". When she finished, I would just bring something else that will distract her from asking me more questions that I couldn't help her with.

As the days went on, with lots of memorising the alphabet, I found myself knowing how to connect a few of the letters and read them. But writing was still a problem. I truly tried, but I couldn't even hold a pen properly. I started reading newspapers and magazine stories. There was a certain man who used to write lots of Swahili stories that were published in different newspapers. I started buying those newspapers to read. Reading those stories really helped me learn how to read. But it was quiet reading. I couldn't read loud for some reasons.

Time passed, and before long it had been nearly two years. That's when the parents of the little boy I was taking care of decided to come back to join their child.

A few days before the arrival of the little boy's parents, the grandmother called me. "My daughter is coming back to take her son so you can start school," she told me.

I couldn't believe what she was saying. I didn't know what to say. I knew she was going to tell me to join secondary school as she had promised two years ago. That same year, the grandmother and her husband opened their own secondary school. So I knew without doubt I was going to join that school. I didn't say anything when the boy's grandmother was talking to me.

Finally the boy's parents came, and they took the boy. I realised there was no turning back. The boy's grandmother was very serious about me starting secondary.

I decided to speak to the little boy's mother and tell her the truth about my school history. "Sister, I have never been to primary school, so I will not be able to join O level," I told her. "Please, can you talk to your mother? If I tell her, she will not understand me."

"What? What are you talking about?" the boy's mother asked.

"Yes, sister, all this time I have been hiding the truth."

"Okay. I will talk to her," she answered.

She went and spoke to her mother.

"Mother said she doesn't want stupidity. You are going to start school," the boy's mother told me.

"But I can't study, and besides, I am too old to start O level," I told the boy's mother.

"That is what she said," she replied.

At that point, I felt like running away, but I didn't have anywhere to go. The boy's mother was concerned as well. She wanted me to take other short courses that I would be able to finish instead of taking O leve for four years. She didn't think I would be able to finish secondary. I real concurred with her because I couldn't figure myself in secondary school. At the time, I was desperate to run from what I had always wanted.

# CHAPTER 11

## You Can Walk above Traditions and Norms Set by Man if You Believe

It was 2003 around eight in the morning. After assembly, I found myself in a class room of eighteen students who knew how to read, write and speak English. By that time, I thought I was dreaming—only to find out this was not a dream but reality. On that day, I felt like I was going to die because my heart was pumping so fast. My hands were shaking and sweating because I couldn't hold a pen. I went to the toilet many times just to hide myself from other student's presence.

I couldn't stop crying, and other students were wondering what was wrong with me. Some students concluded that I didn't want to join school. Some told me to stop crying, saying, "You will get used to school."

"Anyway, it seems to be a good school," one of the students said.

I knew they were thinking that I did not want to join that school. Deep inside, I knew what was troubling me, but I refused to tell them what was in my mind.

When the first teacher came into the class that morning,

he introduced himself and then told us that he wanted us to introduce ourselves by our names and places where we live. All the students before me stood and introduced themselves majestically, seeming to be showing off their ability to speak English. Now it was my turn. I stood up like I knew exactly what I wanted to say. "My name is Gemma , and I came here." Instead of saying my name is Gemma and I live here in Victoria. This is beacause; I was living the same place where the school was.

When I finished speaking, I heard and saw all the students were laughing at me.

"Keep quiet. We are all here to learn. Why are you laughing at her?" the teacher asked.

I felt so ashamed and embarrassed of the fact that I couldn't even make a simple statement that would allow people to understand what I was saying. I felt like I was the stupidest person in the whole class.

Another thing that made me feel embarrassed was the fact that I was the oldest person in the class. Although nobody else knew I was older than everyone else (I think because I was so skinny), I could see clearly that was the case. Knowing that I was the oldest student in the class and yet I couldn't write or read properly pained me greatly. It was difficult to hear the younger students showing off their ability to speak English. While they may not have been able to speak fluently but they were doing their best—and their best was much better than mine. Frankly speaking, everything about the situation was difficult to deal with. Imagine, at the time when I started school, I was already nineteen years old.

On that first day at school, we didn't do much, because it was the opening day. The teachers would come into the classroom just to introduce themselves and tell us what they would be teaching and the things we would need to know about the subjects at hand. Some came with a syllabus, a word whose meaning I did not even know at the time. One teacher brought a syllabus and wanted us to write down few things which were in the syllabus. At that point, I knew I was facing a huge challenge because I didn't know how to write at all.

After the first day in school, I went back home very tired. But I was still a maid (house girl). I had to go back home and do everything that I was supposed to do as a maid. I had to make sure there was food on the table when my bosses come back home. After that, I was supposed to prepare our food as well (I and other few of my employer's relatives). I had so many task that people expected me to do. In the morning, I had to wake up very early to make sure the house was clean and breakfast was on the table before going to school. Imagine what kind of a girl I was supposed to be with such responsibilities.

There was a day I went to school, and I managed to copy down some notes. However, the notes were not neat. So that, in the evening at home, I asked the maid or house girl (the girl who was now taking care of the young boy I had previously cared for) to help me copy the notes properly into another exercise book. She did help me. And for the first time, I had to tell her that I had been told to start this school while I didn't know anything about schooling.

"If you don't even know how to write and read properly, how will it be?" she asked.

"I don't know what to do," I confessed.

When I told her what I was experiencing, she couldn't believe it. For a moment, she didn't say anything. "How can someone who has never been to primary school join a secondary school?" she said after a few minutes of quietness.

"I don't really know," I replied.

"Gemma , don't underestimate yourself. If she thinks you can do it, then you can do it. Just hold on and don't give up," she said, adding, "Gemma , looking at you, I think you can make it. Besides, you are a smart and intelligent girl. I have no doubt you can do it."

"Do you really think I can do it?" I asked her.

"Absolutely, 100 per cent," she answered.

"For the time being, can you help me to copy notes every time I come with the new ones please?" I asked her.

"Yes of course I will help you," she replied.

In addition to agreeing to help me while she was there, she promised to teach me to write as well. At that time, I could at least read a little bit. But writing was still difficult.

Even though she promised to help me, I knew her help wasn't going to last long. At some point, she was supposed to leave there (maid who is now taking care of the boy I cared before)

For the few days she stayed there, she did help me with notes and a little bit of writing. At least I could try to write a little better. And by that time, I had learned more of the alphabet so I could read a little bit more. Finally, it came time when she had to leave. I was now left alone to deal with everything that concerned my studies.

At that time, I was working very hard to learn how to write notes. However, I really didn't know the use of those notes, which we students were taking every day. The teachers and students still didn't understand why I couldn't write and read properly at my age.

One day, we were in the class, and the teacher came to give us notes. One person would write the notes on the board so all the students would copy them. While we were waiting for the person who normally writes on the board,

I heard a loud voice. A student began chanting "Gemma! Gemma! Gemma!"

He was soon joined by other students, cheering for me to go and write the notes on the board. The whole class was waiting to see if I had the guts to go and embarrass myself. That student chose to call me out purposely. He knew very well that I couldn't write properly he just wanted to embarrass me.

They finished making noise, one of the student stood up. This is what he said Gemma's handwriting is like a person who is about to die,"

And everybody started to laugh. I felt badly, but not about the students who were making fun of me. I felt badly about myself. I even started to hate my mother and blame her for not allowing me to go to school. I didn't blame the student. What he had said was true. My handwriting was very bad.

One of my friends took the notes and started to write them on the board.

It was break time, and all students had gone to break. I was left alone in the classroom, continuing taking notes as usual. I was always the last to finish taking notes, because I was so slow to write. One of my favourite teachers came into the classroom. "What are you still doing here?" he asked. "The break is about to finish."

"I am still taking notes," I answered. I had to finish copying the notes. Otherwise, I would not be able to get them, as they were not available anywhere else. When the break finished, the other teacher would come and wipe them away.

"So you are not going for a break?" the teacher asked.

"No," I replied. "I am not going." I xplaine more

"Okay. When you finish, please come to my office. I need to talk to you," the teacher said.

"Okay. I will come," I replied.

I finished and went straight to his office. I was curious to find out what he wanted to talk to me about. He had seemed very concerned about something.

"That was quick. Have a seat," the teacher said as soon as I walked into his office.

I sat down and said, "Yes, teacher. Here I am. I was almost finishing when you came. What have I done?" I asked him. I thought maybe I had done something wrong, so he wanted to tell me off. Normally when the teacher calls you in his or her office, then you know you are in trouble. It wasn't normal for a teacher to call a student into the office unless he or she had something very serious to talk to the student about.

"Gemma , I have called you here to talk to you about your behaviour in class," the teacher explained.

"What behaviour, teacher?" I asked.

"Why do you always cry in class, especially when you are given homework or when you are told to read?" the teacher asked.

Before I answered him, the tears started to roll down my face.

"Gemma , please tell me, what is wrong?" the teacher asked again. He was very concerned for me. I had seen that ever since I started school. He never forced me to do anythingthat I don't want to do in the class. And when I sometimes I couldn't do my homework, he never shouted at me like other teachers, who thought I was not intelligent. Due to that, I decided to tell him the truth.

This is what I said to him. "I wish I could read and write

like other students, but I know it is impossible. I will never be able to do that."

"Why is that impossible?" the teacher asked.

"I have not attended primary school. That's why it's difficult for me to learn anything. I have tried, but I still can't get it right," I explained.

When I finished talking, he looked at me and took a deep breath. "What are you doing here then, if you have not attended primary school?"

"My boss believes I can do it," I replied.

"So do you think you can do O level and pass it?" the teacher asked again.

"I still don't know if I can manage to do that. But I think, as the days go by, my boss may realise I can't continue and take me out of school. That is my prayer," I told the teacher.

The teacher didn't stop there. He asked me another question. "Do you know that next year, you will be sitting for the national exam?"

"National exam!" I was shocked. "What do you mean by national exam?" I asked him.

"This is the exam that will be marked nationally to test whether you are ready to go to another class. If you fail, you will remain in the same class. Those who pass will go to Form 3," the teacher explained to me.

"I real want to know how to write," I told him. "Is there anything you can do to help me with that please? I asked my teacher.

"At this time, you are supposed to be preparing yourself for the big exam, not learning how to write," he said.

My teacher's statement made me know straight away that I wasn't going to make it, no matter what.

"Anyway," he added, "there is a certain exercise book

that has small and big lines in it. Buy it, and I will show you how to learn writing."

I bought the exercise book, and he taught me how to use it. Slowly, my handwriting started to be better.

Days went on, and I even got use to school. I made lots of friends. But still there were some things I didn't understand. For example, there was a day we did a mathematics test. When the results came, I saw that I had scored zero—0 per cent out of 100 per cent. There was another student who other students regarded her as an intelligent girl in the class, scored 50 per cent. This young girl wasn't happy, and I wondered why. I decided to go to ask her.

"Why are you not happy?" I asked.

"I got 50 per cent out of 100 per cent," she answered.

I become confused and lost for a moment. "What do you mean?" I asked.

"My mother will not be happy with me if she finds out I have gotten this marks in mathematics," she said. "How much have you got?"

I opened my paper to show her.

"What? Zero!" she shouted.

But for me I was just laughing. I didn't know what she was talking about, since no one had told me about test results. "How did you get that number 50 per cent?" I asked her.

"I solved few questions. I think that's why I got this small number," she said.

I asked her so many questions about subjects, exams, and how to pass those exams. One of the things she emphasised was the importance of reading books and the notes that we took from the teachers. In addition, she told me it was important to listen attentively to the teachers when they were teaching. She added, "If you do all these things I told you, you will do well in your studies."

After the conversation with Rafina, I became very excited. I wanted to apply all the techniques she had told me to see if her strategy will work.

On the following day, we were having a biology test. The night before the exam, I studded the biology book and the few notes I had managed to take in class. In the morning, I went to school, and we were given the test.

After we had completed it and the results came in, I couldn't believe the score I had received. I had 62 per cent out of 100 per cent. Even the biology teacher couldn't believe it. She had to call me into her office to explain to her how I had done it.

After that result, I knew that if I applied the same technique to other subjects, I would do better in them as well. The happiness of victory felt so good. I had gone from zero to sixty-two. That was a great achievement.

Rafina was so happy to know that she had helped me and that her strategies had worked. Rafina took my result paper, and she started to show it to all the students in class, especially those who had been making fun of me.

The biology result boosted my faith and hope when it came to continuing to pursue school. That day, I went home so happy and excited to show my result to my employer. She was very happy. She had so much faith in me. When I showed her the result, she just smiled and said, "I told you. You will do it. This is just a beginning."

Surely, my handwriting changed completely, and I gained more confidence in my writing skills. But there still a few letters that I couldn't write properly. The letters $K$ and $W$ were the most difficult one for me.

As the days went on with lots of practising, I found

myself in the list of the top five people who had good handwriting in our class. I had gone from being laughed at because of not knowing how to write and read to being noticed for having good handwriting by the same people who had made fun of me. It was incredible. I became so proud of myself, and I became disciplined with the way I used my time. I was determined to make sure that I wouldn't fail Form two.

Although I could now write well, I didn't have speed. I was very slow in writing. Both teachers and students started to tell me that, if I didn't improve my speed, I would not pass the Form two National Exam.

As I mentioned before, the school was new. We had a crisis of teachers leaving, as the school wasn't stable yet. Thus, we were behind on the syllabus, and the Form two National Exam was approaching. I was doing nine subjects. We had only managed to cover aonly two subjects over the whole year. As for the remaining seven subjects, we were just halfway through the syllabus. I became frustrated. At the time, I didn't know what to do.

I decided to ask the teacher who had once helped me learn how to write. I went to talk to him. I knew he had all the answers to my questions about school. "Do you think I can pass the Form two National Exam?" I asked.

He looked at me, and then he said, "Yes, but only if you continue working hard." The expression on his face told a different story. He looked as though he still wasn't convinced that I could do it; he was just saying I could do it so as not to discourage me.

"What can I do to cover the rest of the syllabus? We are so far behind," I asked.

"At this point, you can't cover the syllabus of the remaining subjects, because the remaining time is too short.

But what you can do is to find a way to prepare you for the exam," the teacher answered.

"What are the options?" I asked.

"Review lots. And if you can find a few serious people, make a group discussion. That can help," he answered.

I managed to mobilise a few students, and we started group discussions. A few days after the group discussion had begun, I realised they wouldn't be helpful to me. The discussions were to be held after class hour—at the time I was supposed to go back home to prepare dinner and do other house tasks as a maid. I tried to study after I finish cooking and completing my other tasks. I realised that wasn't going to work either. By then, I was so tired it was difficult to concentrate. Thus, I had to find another mechanism to make sure I would get time to do reviews.

I decided that, after class hours, I would go home straight away and finish up all my responsibilities. Then I would go straight to bed to rest. I could wake up at midnight when everybody was asleep so I could find a quiet place to study. That became my new routine.

I found myself very capable at that time, and my concentration was high because of the quietness.

In the middle of all the pressure, the busyness, and the frustration, I decided to make a small box, which I called the Box of the Covenant—referring to the covenant between me and God. I promised God that I would put any amount of money I get into that box. If He helped me to pass my Form two National Exam, I would give him thanks by giving offering with that money, and I would testify to the church for what He had done in my life. I was faithful. I kept on putting whatever coins or notes I got in the box for that purpose.

As I was in the middle of preparing myself for the exam,

I received very bad news—news that broke my heart. I was informed that my sister had passed away. Since the exam was so near, I did not go home. It was essential that I stayed till I finished my exam.

Days went on. Finally the exam was just around the corner. Two days before the exam, I went to speak to my teacher again. I needed assurance from the person who knew my journey. As we were talking about the exam, I asked my teacher the same question I had asked him nine months ago. "Do you think I will be able to pass the exam that is ahead of me?"

He looked at me again, just like he had the last time I'd asked him that question. "Gemma , you can do it," the teacher answered. But again, I could see that, while his mouth was saying I could do it, his eyes were saying I couldn't. It was the most difficult time I had ever experienced in my life. It seemed as if the whole world was falling on me. I knew there was no way to escape the exam. I told myself that I had to take this exam and I had to pass it. But I didn't know how I was going to do it.

On the first day of the national exam, I was shaking. I did not have enough courage to face the exam. But I prayed that God would give me the courage and faith to face the exam with no fear. I had prepared for all the exams. Unfortunately, a few weeks before the exam, the Ministry of Education had announced that the business subjects would no longer be included in determining the average. I was a bit disappointed, as I knew that the two business subjects (bookkeeping and commerce) were going to add more marks on my exams. At the time, I was doing both well. Finding out about the change caused me confusion, and I felt that all hope of passing was gone. Even before the removal of those subjects, I hadn't been sure whether I was going to make to the next class. With the changes, I knew I was definitely not going to make it.

Nevertheless, I sat for each subject, and finally the exam was over. It was time to wait for the result.

Time went on, and in few months, the results were out. My friend called to tell me that she had heard that the results were out. I told her I hadn't heard anything about the results, adding that I actually didn't want to know; I was so scared to learn that I hadn't made it. She told me I didn't have to worry, as we didn't know anything yet. We would wait till the results were released to our school before we would find out.

Two days later, the results were in our school office. Because I was living close to the school, it was just a matter of few minutes to find out whether I had passed or failed.

I was at home around 3 p.m. when I heard someone knocking on the door. I went to answer it and saw one of my classmates.

"Hey! What are you doing here?" I asked him. We were still waiting for the exam results, so I was surprised to see him there.

"I came to check if our school has received the results, since they are out already," he answered.

"What?" I felt shocked. I couldn't believe what he was saying. "So have you got your results already?" I asked him.

"Not yet," he told me. "But the school secretary is calling you. She said I should call you before she shows me my result."

I became even more scared because I knew she was calling me to tell me about the results.

"Please tell her I am not going," I told him.

"Gemma, come on. Don't be scared. If the results are out, then there is nothing you can do. Just go and find out what you have. For me, I just want to know if I am continuing with school or not. My father told me, if I fail, he is not going to pay for my school fees anymore. I understand him though; this is my second exam. I did last year's exam at my previous school. I failed, which was why I came to this school," he explained.

I did feel sorry for him. But somehow, it seemed as if he was laughing, as if he knew that he had passed. "Okay," I agreed. "Let's go."

We left, heading to the school office.

"Gemma, I called you because I want to send you to the shop," the secretary said.

"What!" I responded. "I thought you'd called me to give me my results. So do you have the results already?" I asked her. I wanted to make sure she wasn't lying because she had promised my classmate that, she will show him the result after he had called me.

I went to the shop, and when I came back, I found my classmate, the one who had come to call on me. He was crying. I didn't even ask what was wrong with him. I knew straight away what the matter was. He had seen his results, and he hadn't made it to the next class.

"Gemma, come and have a look at your results," the secretary said.

"Oh no! I don't want to see it! Can you read it for me please?" I asked the secretary.

"I don't have to read it," she said. "I have seen it already. Well done, Gemma. You have passed."

"What! Are you serious?" I asked her while the tears were coming down.

"Yes. Have a look," she said.

I took the paper that was in her hands to read it. Honestly, I couldn't believe what I was seeing. I had scored

44 per cent, while I only needed 31 per cent, to make it to the next class. I once read a book that said there is peace that transcends all understanding. At that moment, I felt a peace, joy, and happiness I couldn't explain to anyone. I felt alive again. And I realised, little by little, my dreams were coming true. What I had imagined was becoming real. I was so encouraged by my result. At that point I realised if I work hard, I would achieve anything I wanted in life. I knew that, if I wanted to become somebody in life, I would have to work even harder.

My employer was very happy when she found out that I'd managed to go to on the next class. "Gemma, you see. I told you that you were going to make it," she said.

I looked at my employer, and I burst into tears. I saw her as my *hero*. I asked myself the question I had been asking myself over and over—how can a person trust completely someone who had never been to primary school to go to secondary school and succeed?. It is question for which I still don't have the answer today.

Since the results were out, I decided to share with my boss about the Box of the Covenant that I had been keeping and my intention to go to church to give offering of thanks and my testimony.

She told me, "What you want to do is good thing. But why don't you give your offering of thanks for now and then you can give the testimony when you finish Form four because it will be a complete testimony. I believe you will do well in your Form four studies as well."

I had peace in my mind, so I decided to take her advice. I planned to go to church to fulfil one part of what I had promised God. I went to church, and I gave my offering of thanks.

The journey continued. When I entered Form three, I

couldn't believe the number of students who had made it to that class. We were about five of us. The rest repeated the previous class. Some decided to drop school completely because they had failed; they didn't want to go through Nationa Exam any more. In that class, I saw myself as a different person. I had different mindset. I started thinking positive things about myself and even taking myself serious, which was something I had never done before. I started looking at things from a different perspective.

I gained more courage and faith to continue fighting in my studies. I once read a book called *Think Big*. In it, the author, Ben Carson, wrote, "You can do whatever you make up your mind to do." This was a statement I found very encouraging; it helped me during all this time when I was struggling with learning how to write. I knew that, if I make up my mind to do anything, I would do it and achieve something out of it. I knew that, I would complete even Form Four, the last year of secondary school. I will pass Form Four, so I could go on to A levels.

As the days of Form three went on, I continued studying very hard. Because I was so busy, it didn't take long before I realised the year had ended, and I would soon be entering Form four. Again I worked very hard preparing for the final exam. A few months before the Form four National Exam, a mock examination was announced. The mock exam would test to see if we were ready to take the Form four National Exam. When I found out about that, I started spending more time with teachers, asking questions and getting the answers I needed help me prepare for the final exams. My teachers were the only hope for me to do well.

Two weeks before the Form four National Exam, we had a graduation ceremony. It was an emotional celebration, especially for me. I reflected on my journey. At just seven years old, I had become a maid, and now I was celebrating my graduation. I wept on that day. I was also troubled by the fact that the other students and I were going to be a part from each other. Some of them had become like my family, since I had been away from my family for a long time. During the celebration, I was awarded two certificates—the Best Kiswahili Student and the Most Disciplined Student of the Year. I was so happy to receive those two certificates. They truly meant a lot to me. The fact that teachers had acknowledged my hard work made me even happier than I already was.

Finally the Form four National Exam came, and I did it. It took months for the result to come out.

After a long wait, the results were finally available. As usual, it wasn't easy to receive the results. I knew those results would determine my future. Since I was scared to know my result, I decide to give one of my friends a national examination number to check for me. She had already checked hers, and she had passed. This gave me a little hope that I might have passed as well, because the two of us had done few discussion together.

A few minutes after I had spoken with my friend, she rang my phone. But, again since I was scared, I decided not to pick up the call.

As I sat contemplating what to do, I received a text message. I opened it. I couldn't believe the message that I was reading. It read, "Congratulations, my friend. You made it through. You have credits that will take you to A levels."

I shouted out loud with joy and happiness. I rushed to an Internet café to confirm for myself that what my friend had said was true. When I saw the results, I couldn't believe my eyes. I thought maybe I was dreaming. But I thank God it wasn't a dream but a reality.

I became so happy. I could feel that the world was revolving around me. I thanked God for giving me another chance to continue with my higher studies. Since my classmates and I had started Form one, some students had quit. Some had to stop studies when we were in Form two as they could not pass their exams then. Others now had to repeat Form four in order to get the credits that would allow them to join A level studies. And these were people who had been to nursery and primary schools, while I had never been in any basic education. I asked myself so many questions—questions for which I did not have answers at the time.

I went to church to redeem my promise to God. When I first stood in front of the congregation, I could not speak because I was in tears. Eventually, I gained strength and started to speak. By the time I finished, I could see that almost the entire congregation was in tears.

I remember my pastor saying, "I have been born again for so many years, and I have heard so many testimonies. But this one has moved me."

A few weeks later, I received a letter informing me that I had been selected to join government school. I discussed the option with my boss. We agreed that there was no need for me to go far from where I was living, while there was school right there. So instead I joined the same school where I had done my O levels. Deep inside, I wanted to go to boarding school, where I could have a different experience and meet new people. But I didn't have much of a choice or room for argument. I had to agree with my boss (who was also my guardian, as well as my sponsor) to continue at the same school with my A levels.

The A levels were just two years. I met new people and made lots of friends. I enjoyed my A level studies. I was able to study without any pressure, as I understood what I was studying. The subjects were a bit difficult and challenging, but I managed well in comparison to the difficulties I had faced during my O levels.

Later on in my first year, I was elected as a Head girl. I had to adjust myself because I had more responsibilities as a Head girl and student.

A level went by quickly because I was very busy. Finally, we sat for our A level National Examination. I thank God I managed my responsibilities well; in fact, I did so well that, during my final year, I was given an award for the Best Leader of the Year.

On my graduation day, I was very emotional. I knew I was going to be separated from the people I had met in school. On top of that, I was finishing my A level studies, something I had at one point seen as impossible. My friends and few people who knew me were present on that day to witness the occasion, and they were very happy for me.

I was happy, but at the same time, I was nervous. I didn't know whether I was going to pass my exams. Our graduation ceremony was held before the exam.

A few months after my graduation, I travel to Arusha to see my parents and, of course, to break the news that I had finished my A level exams. My parents were very happy, but they did not believe what I was telling them. They knew my background with education, so they were a bit in shock. How a person who had never been to primary school managed to make it straight through both O level and A levels? When they saw my photos of both my O level and A levels graduation ceremonies, they believed what I was telling them.

Few weeks later I went back to Dar res salaam. While I was there waiting for the results of the exams, I had a chance to take a three-month science course. In this course I was taking (mathematics, physics and chemistry). After finishing the course, I went back home to (my employer's house)

Finally, the results came out. I thank God the results were good. Though my expectation was that I would get higher grades than I had gotten, I was grateful that I had passed.

After I'd received the results, I filled out application forms for three different state universities. The selection process took time. Finally the first results came out, and I had not been selected. When this happened, I knew I was not going to join the university, even though I had applied for more than one course and had received no results for even one of the course options.

I started to look for other private universities—relying on faith, as I did not know who was going to pay my fees. While I was waiting to hear back from the universities, I was extremely busy with other stuff. One of the things was writing a business proposal, I desired to open a business that would support me and my family while I was studying at the university. (If I would get a chance to join Unversity)

One day when I was at the Youth International Conference, I received a call from one of the universities that I had applied to, the one that was my first choice. The call was from the university's principal. He told me, "We wrote you a letter, and we have been waiting to hear from you for some time now. But we have not heard anything from you that is why I have decided to call you."

I asked him what was the letter about He told me that I had been selected to take the second course option I had selected on my application. Or if I still wanted to take the first option, which was law, I would have to join the university and take a three-month entry course. Then if I passed that course, I would be accepted into the law course.

I told him I would get in touch with the university within two days. I was very happy. However, before receiving the news, there was a suggestion that I might go abroad to live and study there to the (family whose child I had previously taken care of). I went home the same evening to tell my boss the news.

I was filled with excitement as I talked to her about going to university. She kept quiet for some time, and then she took a deep breath. "How about the option of going abroad?" she asked.

I kept quiet. I could not say anything. Deep inside, I did not want to go to abroad. I had my own ambitions—things that I wanted to accomplish while I was in my country.

After the conversation with her, I knew there was nothing I could do to change her mind. Nevertheless, I decided to take another alternative to try to convince her. I spoke to the two sisters (my employer's daughter and niece) the niece was living there with us while the daughter was married and lived somewhere else. I asked them if they would try to convince and change my boss's mind for me not going to Europe but it did not work out.

By that time, I had already applied for the new passport because the previous one had expired. So my hands were tied. I had no way of getting myself to university, though I very much desired to go.

Anyway, my passport came, and immediately I applied for the visa. When I was waiting for the visa, my heart was troubled. I spoke to my friends who had been selected to join different universities and were waiting to start their studies; this made me very uncomfortable. Very few people knew what was going on with me. As for the rest of my friends, when they asked me what university I was going to, I would tell them I wasn't going to any university, as I was waiting on something. I did not want to tell them that I was going abroad, because I was not sure that I was going to get the visa. This was a painful experience again. I had to start being positive and to pray for my visa application to be accepted to avoid disappointment and shame.

As I was waiting for the visa, I received a call from my friend who had been accepted at a certain university. She told me that the second selection was out and she had seen my name. She encouraged me to go to an Internet café to check. When I checked and found my name, I felt badly. I knew wasn't even going to mention it to my boss.

Among the few people that I told about my plans of going to Europe, many didn't want me to go overseas because they wanted me to study there. On the other hand, a few friends of mine were telling me that I was so lucky to get the opportunity to go abroad. Gemma so many people are praying day and night to get this opportunity just go. One of my friend told me.

Within a short time, I got my visa. It took just two weeks, and I was supposed to travel within a few days of receiving the visa. So suddenly, I became very busy. I had to travel to Arusha to say goodbye to my father and mother and make all other preparations for the journey. My parents were so happy that their daughter was going to Ulaya (Europe). They had no idea that I was not happy; I did not show them. I only stayed there for two days then I had to go back to Dar res salaam, on the way coming from Arusha I remembered about Liz and Asa (Asa the man who once attempted to rape me) I decided since the wife was very good to me and the children I would go to see them before I go to Europe.

Asa and Liz lived just a walking distance from where I

was living. It was evening when I arrived at Liz and Asa's house. I knocked the gate and a maid came to open for me. As she saw me she started crying and hugged me so tight. As we were still hugging Joshua came running toward where we were standing.

Hello Joshua. I greeted him.

Hello sister. He answered while hugging.

Where is your mother? I asked Joshua.

There on the sky! Joshua said pointing on the sky.

What do you mean? I asked.

My mother went to God. Joshua added.

What is going on Asha? I asked the maid (we knew each other because she took over from me when I was about to get married, I inducted her before I left to Arusha)

Liz died three month later after you left. Asha answered.

What! I said with shock.

What happened to her? I asked Asha.

She found out her husband had incurable disease (H IV) so she couldn't take it she died with shock. Asha explained. I couldn't believe everything that was happening. I started to think about myself. Reflecting about the day that Asa attemted to rape me, what if he had managed to rape me that could mean I would be waiting for my death as well. This whole thing reminded me about Nyanjege (the maid I took over from, who died and who warned me about Asa though she didn't tell me direct). I left Liz's house very sad and feeling very sorry for the children whom now they didn't have a mother.

It was a Sunday, the morning of 10th January 2010, when I went to the airport. As I waited to check in, I heard someone calling my name. I turned and saw it was my boss's husband.

"Yes, Dad," I said.

He said to me, "We thank God He used us to accomplish what He wanted us to accomplish in your life. Go my daughter and prosper." He spoke again. "Know the times and seasons of God in your life and work accordingly, then you will prosper."

I did not understand that statement at the time but now I know what he meant.

In a few hours, the plane took off. It took some hours to reach my final destination. I landed the same day. The following day, I went to the college to finish the process and all the paperwork I would need to start at the college. Initially, I was supposed to start certificate level courses. But when my host saw my previous qualification, he told me that I qualified to start diploma level. So we contacted the course awarding body.

A few days later, the awarding body replied. I had been accepted to start a diploma level one.

I started my course, but I was bit scared. I knew my exams would be marked by people who didn't know my background, especially my history with English. I knew it would be difficult. I was encouraged as the days went by, as I started to grasp all the subjects I was studying.

We would sit for exams twice a year. So from Diploma level one to Advanced Diploma, I was supposed to take three years to finish. By God's grace, I finished within two years.

After I finished this course, I realised that it was not about knowing English or attending primary school. Rather, it was about dedication; passion; determination; and, most of all, discipline. You have to be disciplined in everything you do; otherwise, you will never achieve any goal in life. Knowing who you are and finding something to live for are the most important things in life. There was a time in my life when I had wanted to give up. But I knew that, if I did, nothing would change in my life and in the lives of the people I cared about.

For example, when I started O level, the first year was incredibly difficult for me. I found everything that was happening strange. Learning how to read and write was the most difficult thing I had ever experienced. I wanted to quit. But told myself that, if I quit, my younger sister would end up be the same as me at the time (a house girl), and she would pass through what I had passed through. I did not want that to happen. I had to work hard so that I would be able to finish my studies and get a job. I wanted to help my family, particularly my younger sister, whom I loved so much. I wanted her to have a chance to go to school and be somebody one day.

Because of my sister, I kept fighting in life. This taught me a big lesson—in this life, if you have something to live for, you will be able to fight anything that comes your way.

Another thing I have learned in my life is the importance of being faithful and innocent like a child. Then you will get rewards in life. The rewards might not come from the person you have been faithful to, but they will surely come to you in one way or another. I remember when I was still a house girl the way my bosses were treating me. I wished I could be rude and bad to their children when they were not around. But there was a certain voice inside telling me these were just children. They didn't understand what their parents were doing to me. They were innocent angels.

So I never mistreated any of my boss's children because their parents treated me badly. Even for the wives who treated me badly, when their husbands wanted to sleep with me, I declined. I could have accepted so that I could hurt them the way they were hurting me. Yet I didn't do that. I knew it was wrong. I always put myself in the wives' shoes, imagining how I would feel if someone was sleeping with my husband. In addition, l knew that, if I planted bad things, then bad things would come back to me. So I learned to be faithful and honest to every house I lived in.

I can boldly say that life has rewarded me with a wonderful husband and two beautiful and intelligent girls. I am living happily with my family in the United Kingdom. The journey of my destiny continues, as the best is yet to come!

# AUTHOR BIOGRAPHY

Gemma is an inspiring new author. Through her writing, she gives hope, ignites dreams, and encourages people from rough backgrounds to press on and fight for their new better tomorrow.

Running from a family ordeal at a very young age, she worked as a maid for over twenty years. It is remarkable that, through faith and hope for a better future, Gemma defied the odds. With no formal primary education, she managed to obtain a secondary education and became a graduate and associate member of the Association of Business Executives (ABE) and she continues pursuing other aspirations.

She is now married, is blessed with two beautiful girls, and lives in England.